T0196089

TWO **PATHS** ONE UNDERSTANDING

JIM COUNTER AND ANNA COUNTER

BALBOA.
PRESS

A DIVISION OF HAY HOUSE

Balboa Press books may be ordered through booksellers or by contacting

Balboa Press
A Division of Hay House
1663 Liberty Drive
Bloomington, IN 47403
www.balboapress.com
1 (877) 407-4847

Print information available on the last page.

ISBN: 978-1-9822-1910-9 (sc)
ISBN: 978-1-9822-1911-6 (e)

Balboa Press rev. date: 12/21/2018

Contents

Jim's Story

Jan's Story

Jim's Foreword

My sister, Jan, and I have been talking for several years about writing a book together. I am seventy-four years young, and Jan is my older sister. (It's not polite to tell a lady's age.) I have enjoyed a most wonderful life in this go-around, and my children have encouraged me to document some of my experiences and beliefs. I have had a successful career as a financial advisor and life insurance salesman, but even though this is not a story about my career path, the experiences I have had serving my clients over the last forty-nine years have helped to form my beliefs.

Jan's life has not been as blessed as my own, and even though we have the same parents, our life experiences in this incarnation have been very different. Although we have lived apart since I was ten years old, our spiritual bond has always remained, pulling us ever closer.

Jan channels an entity called Romulus as well as some others. They are working on a project that involves the lifting of the curtain between our current human existence and our true spiritual selves on the other side. Romulus and the other entities have been telling Jan for several years that she and I would be writing a book together. At first I was a little doubtful, as she is a published author and I have no experience in writing. Jan has a huge vocabulary and I—not so much.

We could not agree on how to put our separate experiences together, even though the outcomes of these experiences have put our beliefs in the same place. We decided to keep our own separate writing styles and complete the book in two parts. Now, with two strong-willed incarnates, whose part would go first? That was decided with the flip of a coin.

This book will be about the God Source, a title which follows from the quantum definition of life. While it will not be about religion, it will be about spiritual beliefs. I have found that if people have just a little inclination in this direction and an open mind, they may find the subjects of this book of interest.

This is the story of our beliefs and our sense of possibilities. Take from it what you wish, and whatever doesn't feel right with you—just leave it there. We hope you enjoy.

Jan's Foreword

Schoolhouse Earth—A Class in Our Forever Lives

> And the day came when the risk to remain tight in a bud
> was more painful than the risk it took to blossom.
> —Anaïs Nin

These profound words explain my search that is forever ongoing, and the gradual transformation of my life and my worldview. I have changed core beliefs over and over again as my life's search has led me over mountains and down roads that sometimes gave up their knowledge readily. Other times, there were deep rivers and frightening swamps that caused me to wonder whether this life was worth seeing to its end. The quest has, however, kept me always going forward as I sought what is out there just beyond my sight. I believe that I have discovered reasons and hopefully gained some wisdom as to why I am here and why I chose the paths that resulted in my writing this book.

I have always had a thirst to know more and to understand everything that caught my interest. Early on, I started asking questions. Is there really a God? If so, what does He look like? Will I go to Hell if I lie? If there is a God, why does He seems to love some people more than others? As I grew older and my knowledge increased, I progressed to more involved questions and more powerful fears. Has there ever been a time when we have known for certain who and what we really are? What makes us tick? What makes up our reality? Are we just accidents, and do our lives hold no more meaning than bacteria growing on the surface of a planet? Did we invent a God and a Heaven in order to feel that we are not alone in the vastness of space and to assure ourselves that there is a caring creator if we obey the rules? Do we need a God image to design for us an acceptable form of right and wrong? Did we invent the Devil as a foil to this God to teach us that if we did right, we would go to a wonderful place called Heaven, and that if we did wrong, according to accepted beliefs, there would be horrible punishment in an opposite place called Hell? What is our individual conception of how and why we're here?

The deist uses reason to explain God, yet others are willing to build their beliefs on what they see as gospel or divine revelation. Monotheists believe in the one God; polytheists believe in many gods. Agnostics are not sure that there is a God and believe there is no way of proving God's existence or nonexistence. Atheists profess a total nonbelief in any god whatsoever.

Organized religions are wonderful guides as far as they go, and yet each has a particular and often different path up the mountain of life. They all teach certain values to live by that they believe to be God's will and God's entire will. The different religions, however, do not have the whole album of God's will, merely one snapshot. Their paths often cross in agreement, yet each seems to have the idea that its road is the only road to the true God. Is there a way to combine all facets of our reality to form a concept that will explain the wondrous miracle of our lives in this physical reality, a concept that will satisfy all the principles and standards that have separated individual beliefs for so long? With the advent of quantum physics, we now have a way to explain many of the enigmas that have preoccupied so many of us in trying to explain God and the reason for our existence.

So many questions—and I am still asking them. I look back and try to decide if I have ever found any real answers, and you know, I can't say that I have. Whenever I congratulated myself on a seeming step forward, I would look closer and what I saw turned out to be not an answer but only another road leading me further onward in my journey toward truth. Our perceptions are always formed by our life experiences, and our beliefs of the moment are always formed by our perceptions. It is no wonder that as I explored my mind for the meaning of truth current beliefs changed often and, at times, radically and as my perceptions changed my beliefs followed suit. I think of my journey as finding a way through the maze of my present life while being constantly led further into a reality that is being made known piece by small piece—a reality that changes as each piece finds its place in this puzzle that is mortality.

There are times in people's lives when they ask themselves, "Is this all there is?" Well, there have been many such times in my life, and it seems that each time I asked myself that question, the very fact that I did ask led me to another breakthrough in my continuing search for truth. Each time I examined my beliefs about what reality actually meant to me, I found they had expanded. The itch was always there—the need to know more, the need to examine each new concept and place it in context to form an expanded version of "TRUTH." I find that no matter how much I search and study and open my mind to new thoughts and ideas, I am never satisfied. After so many years of mining each new concept for truth, it seems that I have barely scratched the surface. Yet these pages will attempt to document a life spent making the right—and often wrong—decisions that finally led me to the personal truths that, for now, shape my beliefs.

The chance of finding the "incredible," the "astounding," the "miraculous," the "truth" is what has kept me probing reality trying to solve this mystery we call life.

Jim's Story

Chapter 1

In the Beginning

I am sure I am not the first to wonder about the story of creation. This subject has caused me to think and study for most of this life. My sister, Jan, and I have been discussing creation and God almost since the first memories of my current life began. We were raised to be spiritual but not in a specific religion. This book will not be about any specific religious beliefs but rather about personal experiences that have formed my understanding of who I am and where I came from.

Jan and I started this life being born to monetarily poor but spiritually endowed parents who helped us form our curiosity about life itself. When I was five years old and Jan was nine, our parents divorced. We stayed with Mom, as was the tradition at the time. Dad accepted employment with an international construction firm and spent several years working on the big international airport in Reykjavik, Iceland. When he returned to the United States, he got a job at Allis-Chalmers in West Allis, Wisconsin, a suburb of Milwaukee. Because of this we didn't see him for most of our formative years.

Mom moved us to a very poor area of Minnesota onto an old farm where she had lived during her childhood. This farm had been homesteaded by her grandparents and had remained in the family over the years. Electricity had not yet been extended to the area by the Rural Electric Association, so we lived with kerosene lamps and a wood stove for cooking and heating. The toilet was a small two-holer in the back yard well away from the house, for obvious reasons. Our cabin was on the banks of the Mississippi River, so you might say we had a house with a view. Our drinking water was taken directly from the river, which allowed our bodies to build up immunities to many of the common bugs that we have today.

I did mention that we were raised spiritually, so let me explain what I mean by that statement. Mom was a great teacher of life. She would take me into the woods and tell me about all of the trees and plants and animals. She knew the names and uses of each one. She knew which ones were edible and which were not, or even poisonous. The main thing Mom taught was respect for life. Not just human life, but of all life, from the plants in the woods to the clams in the river. She taught me that all life has a place in this world and that we are always to respect each piece of life. She explained that our sustenance is a gift from other lives so we might survive and thrive. She taught us to be thankful for each meal made of these gifts so freely given by the life of the plant or animal we were consuming.

Mom also taught us to respect other humans without prejudice for their race or position. She said all life was loved by God, and even though we were monetarily poor, God would not give us more challenges than we could handle. Mom also instilled in us the love of reading and learning. She had memorized a great deal of poetry and often would recite it to us while she was cooking a meal. Both Jan and I became voracious readers, and we loved to read about places and things we would never be able to experience (or so we thought).

In those formative years I learned principles that I have lived by for my entire life, such as "Always leave a place better than you found it," and "You can be anything you want to be if you believe you can."

When Mom met a man with four small children, we moved in with them all soon after. The youngest of the children was just a few weeks old, and the oldest was five. The mother of our stepbrothers and stepsisters left within weeks of our moving in, never to return. Now Jan and I were the oldest in a family of six children. Mom always said she had enough love for everyone, and she proved that by being fair to all of the siblings—everyone except Jan, who always seemed to be the one who got in the most trouble. As I matured and had children of my own, I realized that the oldest child is the one who trains the parents and paves the way for the younger siblings. (My oldest son, Scott, will testify to that.)

The eight of us lived on a small dairy farm, and there I learned a work ethic that has pretty much stayed with me my whole life. At age seven I was milking cows by hand twice a day, and I even learned how to drive the tractor. I would cut trees in the woods with a handsaw and drag them home, and then split them into firewood for both the cookstove and our barrel stove heater. (A barrel stove is nothing but a fifty-five-gallon barrel with legs attached and a door at one end that allows feeding of firewood.)

My stepfather, Leo, was gone all week in the summer, coming home only for weekends, so Mom and I had to take care of the farm. In addition to milking the cows, we had to cut the hay and haul it into the barn for feed for the cows in the winter. The summers were always the busiest time of the year. I sometimes thought that Leo worked away from the farm because it was easier for him, but I know now that the farm alone did not provide the necessary income for the family.

Jan, being the oldest, would have to take care of the younger children, the house, and a lot of the garden. We maintained a very large garden, from which Mom canned between six and seven hundred quarts of food each year. We would also pick wild berries that she made into preserves. We had to buy the staples like flour and sugar from the store, but the rest of our food was raised and canned in quart jars. Sometimes we could afford a crate of peaches or cherries in season, which she would can up for special treats in the winter.

We still had a two-hole outhouse. I could never understand why they made it with two holes, because people never used it in tandem. The toilet paper was an old Sears catalog. The shiny pages survived the longest.

We raised chickens and hogs for meat and would butcher a steer when we had one. We did not have a refrigerator or freezer, so Mom would have to can all of the meat in Mason jars. Those jars were a scarce commodity, so you can understand why butchering had to be spaced out. Fortunately, my stepfather was an excellent hunter and provided venison, squirrels, woodchucks, and fish (not always in season) for the times when we were out of canned meat. We were also able to get government surplus potatoes, rice, and beans from the county when they were available.

Though we were poor, I did not realize it because many of our neighbors were in the same position we were. There was no television to show us how the rest of the world lived, so we were content. Milking the cows by hand each morning before I went to school and again when I got home before supper was a great experience for learning a work ethic, but our way of life also carried with it some disadvantages. We had no indoor bathroom, and our tub was made of galvanized steel and rested on the floor. We would usually take a bath once a week. Mom would heat the water in the old copper boiler on the stove and in the stove's water reservoir. We all had to use the same water, so you can understand why we would argue for early positions in the tub.

Can you imagine going to school directly from the cow barn without a shower, wearing the same shoes you had on when you cleaned the barn? (We could afford only one pair each.) My classmates always kept their distance, and there were times when the teacher would have to put my desk in a separate area so the kids would stop complaining of the smell. That was very humbling, but I think it also helped me to form my attitude and desires for my future. I must say that the experience did not afford long-term friends, because I seldom had any.

We moved around a lot. I changed schools nine times in my first eight years of school. We could not afford to pay the rent on the farms we lived on, so we were evicted on a fairly regular basis. Sometimes we would move onto an abandoned farm without the absentee owners' knowledge. Sooner or later the owners would find out we were living there and evict us, but we got to live there sometimes for a year or two before they found out. Moving in itself was quite an experience. We did not have a lot of possessions, but we would have to move our few farm animals by herding them down the road to the place we were moving to. To hire a truck to move the animals was a financial impossibility.

Some of the schools I attended were rural schools where all eight grades were in one room. At the Longfellow School we had an average of three students per grade. It must have been a real challenge for the teacher to have lesson plans for eight different classes and teach them all in the same room. We did have fun in school, always looking forward to recess so we could play softball or antiover. Antiover was a game where we would divide into two teams, one on each side of the schoolhouse. One team would holler "antiover" and throw a softball over the schoolhouse roof. The opposing team would then have to spot the ball and catch it. The team that caught the most balls in the series was the winner.

By the time I was twelve I had become an efficient farm worker and had grown strong and skilled. One fall night I forgot to drain the radiator on the tractor and it froze, breaking the water pump. My stepfather was away working at the time, and I knew I was in for something bad when he got home at the end of the week. Mom went to town and bought a new water pump, and I took the tractor apart and replaced the pump before my stepfather got home. He was still quite upset, but not as much as if he'd had to replace it himself.

Sometimes I was even loaned out to other families. When I was thirteen, Jack, one of Mom's friends, broke his leg as he was skidding out logs from the woods with his team of horses. Mom moved me in with Jack and Em to help them with their small dairy farm. Jack could not help much, as his leg was in a cast from his hip to his toes. I would milk his six cows in the morning before I went to school, and when I got back in the evening I would clean the barn, feed the cows, and milk them again. Em was a very heavyset jovial woman who would never go into the barn. She was a great cook though, and I got to eat all I wanted rather than having to share portions with my stepbrothers and sisters. I truly felt like I was in fat city.

One day I when I was out in Em and Jack's strawberry patch, I found a garter snake. As I looked around, I saw snakes all over. There was a metal bushel basket there, so I put about a dozen snakes into it. The snakes could not get out of the basket, but they kept trying to come up the sides, a dozen snake heads reaching for the top. I carried the basket of snakes up to the kitchen door and asked Em to come outside. She came out, but then she started screaming, slamming the door and telling me in no uncertain terms that I was never to come into her house again. I went about my chores, but when it came to suppertime, Em would not let me come in to eat. Jack took a plate of food to me out in the barn, where I stayed for the night. The next day Em felt sorry for me and let me back in the house.

Chapter 2

An Unexpected Move

Jan is four years older than I am, and our life paths diverged fairly early. She got Mom's permission to get married at age sixteen to a twenty-something man, who promptly moved her away to southeastern Iowa. Jan was concerned about me and told me that I should leave the home place too. I wasn't living there much anyway, and she wanted me to move in with my father. She had shared with Dad some of the experiences I had gone through, and he was not happy about that, so they decided to try and remove me from Mom's care.

Dad lived in Milwaukee and was employed as a coil winder by Allis-Chalmers Manufacturing Company. I didn't know him very well, as I had only seen him four or five times since the divorce that happened when I was five. Our first visit was when I was eight. He sent bus and train tickets so I could come and see him in Milwaukee. He would never send cash because Mom always got the mail, and he knew she would convince me that the money was necessary for the family. In retrospect it was, but that never seemed to affect her and Leo's ability to spend money at the local tavern.

There was a lot of strife in our life in those days. I will always remember one day for its especially high level of violence. Leo was later than normal coming home from work on a Friday night. He had stopped at the local tavern to cash his check and have a beer. Mom had been working with me in the hayfield and was looking forward to going out for a beer too. She was extremely upset because he had gone to the tavern without her, and an argument ensued. He threw a wad of cash at her while she was milking a cow. It landed in a pile of sloppy manure in the gutter. This really made her mad, so she fished it out and said she was leaving for the tavern without him.

She got in our only car and started down the road. Leo ran and got the deer rifle, which was always loaded. He was a very good shot and aimed to hit the gas tank. But by the time he got a shot off, she was almost a quarter mile away and his shot was a little high, hitting the trunk instead and lodging in the back seat. Mom furiously drove back into the yard. By this time Leo had gotten on the tractor, and he drove it into the car. He still had the rifle. Mom got out of the car, grabbed the rifle from him, and swung it at him with enough force to break the stock when it hit the tractor. She then proceeded to throw the rest of the rifle out into the middle of the Mississippi River. I was twelve at the time, and had been milking my cows, so I witnessed the entire scene from the barn. My four younger stepbrothers and sisters were cowering in the house, also watching everything. Needless to say, they were terrified. We all, however, knew enough to stay out of the way. Mom and Leo then seemed to settle down and drove off to the tavern together. I finished milking the cows after quieting the kids down. There was no money for repairs, so we just continued to drive the dented car with a bullet hole in it.

Mom was not in favor of my trip to Milwaukee, but because I already had the tickets, she decided to let me go. She took me the bus depot in Aitkin where I boarded a Greyhound bus to Minneapolis. I then took a cab to the Milwaukee Road train depot and got help from the Travelers Aid desk to get me on the correct train. When I arrived, Dad was still at work, so I had to get a taxi to Smitty's Restaurant in West Allis, where I waited many hours for him to get off work at 11:40 pm. We spent a few days together before he again sent me back to Aitkin. Today parents would be criticized for letting an eight-year-old travel alone, but I loved it and felt very grown up.

Dad told me he would like me to come and live with him. He said I would be able to go to the movies and eat in restaurants, so it seemed like a great life to me. I didn't get to do either back home. But living with Dad was not even in my realm of possibility. Back then it was extremely difficult to transfer custody of a young child from a mother to a single father. Also, I was only eight at the time, and unaware that in Minnesota the courts took into consideration the child's wishes at age fourteen. And I just knew that Mom would never allow me to leave her, the only home I had ever had, even though Jan had told me that Dad really wanted me and that she was working with him to have that happen. (I never shared that part with Mom because I didn't want to hurt her or make her mad.) As time passed I forgot about going to live with Dad, unaware that Jan and Dad were continuing to make plans for my removal.

I was thirteen when I started working for Jack and Em. I really liked working there because they always praised me and I had the best food that I had ever eaten in my life. I could also eat as much as I wanted. I was in the seventh grade and the school bus picked me up right at their driveway. That was a lot better than having to walk a mile to catch the bus from home.

I still had to milk and care for cows, and I was lonely for the family, but the pros of being at Jack and Em's outweighed the cons. Jack paid me, but that went directly to Mom to help support the family. I quite literally never had even a nickel for a treat at the store near our school in Aitkin. My dad, on a couple of occasions, sent a five-dollar bill to Uncle Charlie to give to me. Charlie would come over to the house and talk to Leo, positioning himself between us. He would slide up his jacket, exposing the bill sticking out of his rear pocket. I could then snatch it without Mom or Leo knowing. The first time this happened I felt very rich. I took the money to school and went to the drugstore and ordered a butterscotch sundae. I felt so guilty about it that I gave the rest of the money to Mom.

One night at Jack and Em's, quite to my surprise, Jack came into my room and woke me up, saying that Mom was there and wanted me to come with her, right now. On the way home she told me she had received a summons to have me appear in court the following day. She wanted to know what the hell was going on and why I never told her I was planning on leaving her. Truth be known, I did not know what was going on, other than what my sister had told me much earlier about Dad wanting to get custody of me. Both Mom and I were awake all night. She was crying and I was feeling selfish and guilty for hurting her.

The next day was the first time I had ever been in court. I was just fourteen. The judge heard arguments on both sides, but I think his decision to transfer my custody to my dad was made when my Uncle Charlie and Uncle Irven got up (my mom's brothers) and told the following story about an experience I had when I was eleven: "One evening right after supper Jim went out to the barn to do the milking. At that time they were milking twelve cows, so he was supposed to milk six and his stepfather the other six. He was finishing his fourth cow by the time the stepfather started on his. Jim finished up and the stepfather told him he had to milk some of his cows. Jim told him no and started for the house. The stepfather stopped Jim and repeated his demand. Jim pointed out that if the stepfather had come out to milk earlier, he could have milked his own cows, and again said no. The stepfather then took him down on the barn floor and forced some cow dung into his mouth. Jim said he still would not milk the damn cows."

After the judge heard this story, he awarded custody to my dad. On that day my whole life changed, along with one of my potential futures. I went home and packed the few things I had into a cardboard box and left for a new and different life—an experience that was scary and exciting at the same time. While farming would remain in my blood, this decision removed me from physical participation in farming for the rest of my entire life.

Chapter 3

From Farm to City

At the time, Jan lived in Muscatine, Iowa, with her husband and daughter. I went to stay with them for the summer, knowing I would move to Milwaukee before school started in the fall. When I arrived, my sister noted that I had a large ringworm patch on my left arm, about the size of an orange. At home we could never afford to go to a doctor, so I was treating it with a home remedy that required me to use a sharp toothpick to open each of its many blisters, followed by a generous application of merthiolate, a mercury compound. Needless to say this was not a pleasant experience. Jan took me to the doctor and he gave me some salve that cured the ringworm, painlessly, in just a few days. I was very impressed.

My summer with Jan was ever so nice. She cooked things I had never eaten at home, and they were delicious. (It took some getting used to. How was I to know that you weren't supposed to eat the tails of the shrimp?) If you are beginning to think I am motivated through my stomach, you are probably right.

At first it was difficult to get used to all the free time. There were no cows to milk, no barn to clean, and no wood to cut. I learned that I really could sleep after 5 in the morning. Jan had a 21-inch black-and-white television. I had never seen TV and became addicted right away, especially to *Howdy Doody* and *The Mickey Mouse Club*. Like most boys at that time, I developed a huge crush on Annette Funicello.

Jan gave me an allowance, so I was able to go down to the drugstore and have cherry Cokes. This was another new treat for me, and I loved it. My palate was being enhanced, never to return to the simpler diet. I am not saying that the new diet was healthier, but it certainly contained more variety and a broader spectrum of tastes.

When I lived on the remote farm in northern Minnesota, I never had the opportunity to form a close friendship with anyone my own age. It was also partly because we moved so often and I had to change schools almost every time we moved. Jan lived in the middle of town, so I was able to meet and form relationships with several young people. I met a guy that I spent a lot of time with just walking and talking. We became close friends and passed many happy days finding new adventures. I will always remember the experiences I had that summer as the beginning of my future. I began to formulate a whole new definition of what that future could be like.

But, alas, fall came and I had to leave Jan, the only thread connecting me to my former life. On to Milwaukee! To a Dad I didn't know. Although I was looking forward to this new adventure, I had a few reservations and fears. I would have to get used to a new parent. Would he be mean and strict, or would he be fun and gentle and have empathy for my age group? Another new school. At least I would not smell like a cow barn. I had gotten used to a real bathtub at Jan's and had been using it on a daily basis. Dad had sent Jan some money to buy me some new clothes, so I was looking forward to school and being a part of the "normal" group for the first time.

Dad had been living in a single room above a tavern in West Allis, but after I was there a few days he rented a small apartment with one bedroom, a kitchen, a living room, and a half bath. We had to use the landlady's bathroom downstairs to take a bath. So much for that daily routine. She was a water conservationist (as well as anything else that cost money.) We had to come in the back door and go through her kitchen to get up to our apartment. I was to find out the disadvantage of that arrangement very soon. She was an old widow lady who had nothing to do but monitor my comings and goings and anyone I brought home with me.

I quickly became the "house ape," doing the cooking, cleaning, and washing our clothes in the landlady's washing machine. (Thank you, Mom, for teaching me all of that.) I would mow the lawn, shovel the snow, and do anything Mrs. Rauche asked me to do, drawing on my lifelong farm work ethic. I also got to know the neighbor by helping him with different chores around his home. He always told me I would make some girl a good wife some day. He was especially impressed when I hung our clothes out on the line to dry (the landlady did not have a clothes dryer.)

Dad worked from 3 in the afternoon until 11 at night at Allis-Chalmers. We rarely saw one another. I was at school when he woke up and in bed by the time he returned home. (Sometimes, I did manage to squeak in the door just a very few minutes before he did.) This was a very lonely time in my life. I missed my mother and my sister and the family life I had grown up with. For every negative there seems to be a positive though. While the lack of family contact made me lonely, it did provide me with opportunities that most kids don't have. And yes, while my use of some of those opportunities may not have been approved by most parents, I did learn to become self-sufficient.

I had never had any close relationships with the opposite sex (except in my fantasies). The second night at Dad's, he gave me money and said I could go to a show after dinner. This was another first for me: having money and eating out on my own. I had only gone to the movies two other times in my whole life. Now I was living high. As I walked down Greenfield Avenue on the way to the show, a girl my age asked me if I lived around here. I told her that I had just moved here yesterday. I was mostly tongue-tied because I had never talked to a girl one-on-one before. She must have felt sorry for me, because she asked me if I would take her to a movie. I thought taking her with me to the movie seemed a much better choice than taking myself out to dinner, so I agreed. After the show she let me walk her home, and we sat and talked for a long time in the alley behind her house. This was the first time I got to touch a girl's breast. Even though it was through clothing, it was a terribly exciting experience.

The next day Dad taught me another life lesson. I related everything that had happened the night before and he blew up at me, saying this was a totally unacceptable thing to do and I should be ashamed of myself. In actuality, I felt pretty good about it all, and the lesson I learned was that we do not share all of the details of our experiences with others (particularly fathers).

As the days went by I continued to long for the intimate conversations with my mother and sister that I had been used to. Dad and I had very few conversations, and they were limited mostly to the weekends. I truly believe that this was one of the contributing factors to my being open to self-exploration, open to thoughts of creation and why we are here. With so much time at my disposal, I began to read for the pure pleasure of it.

I also spent a lot of time doing homework. We did not have television, computers, or any kind of electronic gadgetry, so I had plenty of time to read for extra credit in my classes, and I loved mathematics. I excelled in most of my classes and was on the honor roll. With all the praise I received from my teachers, I was able to expand my self-image in a positive direction.

I had always been able to hold conversations with adults, and I liked and was liked by my teachers. While this quickly got me the reputation of being a brown-nose, it also taught me a lifelong truth: "Life is like a mirror; you get out of it exactly what you put into it." This one lesson formed my overall outlook on life. We might change the word "mirror" to "Universe," which would vastly broaden the meaning: "Whatever we project into the mirror of the Universe will come back to us."

I am sharing with you some of my early experiences so you will know that I was not a particularly strange, "woo-woo" kid—rather, my experiences were similar to those most of you have had at one time or another. Most, if not all, of my beliefs to date are a compilation of every one of my life events. It is my belief that you as an individual are also an exact reflection of your experiences to date. (Be aware also that some of those experiences may not be from this particular incarnation.)

I have found throughout my life that I can control what happens to me, and around me, with my thoughts. I can be happy or sad based simply on what I am thinking about. Mind you, I am not saying that I can change others in any way, but I can change myself by creating my own interpretation of my surroundings. For instance, we cannot change the temperature in the air around us, but we can change how we react to it.

Let me relate an experience that helped me form my beliefs. In Milwaukee, one of the coldest places you can be in the winter is downtown with a damp wind howling off Lake Michigan. I was standing on the corner of Wisconsin Avenue and Water Street waiting for the light to change. I was so cold that the muscles in my neck and back were tight and hard. I willed them to relax, and found myself feeling warmer. At that moment I realized I could control how my body reacts to the cold. Day after day I would test this out, leaving my coat open. Eventually I didn't need an overcoat, even when the temperature dropped below zero. I learned that things only bother us if we let them.

We all have many experiences like this that we can observe closely and then learn from. I could have just chalked it all off to coincidence and forgotten it. Instead I learned to use my new knowledge of my body's sensory control. For many years after that I very seldom wore an overcoat, even on the coldest winter days, unless I was going to be outdoors for a long time.

Monks in the high altitudes of Tibet have been observed to demonstrate their sensory control by removing most of their clothing and stepping outside in freezing cold weather. They then lie down on cold rocks with only a wet blanket covering them for the entire night. Witnesses have reported what looks like steam rising from the blankets. When the monks wake up in the morning, the blankets are dry.

We all have that control over our own bodies. Our spirit, or mind, can cope with any physical experience because our mind is eternal, while our bodies are temporary. We are constantly evolving as a human and as a spirit. Many of you have read, or at least heard of, a book called *The Secret*. Its authors describe our ability to control what we become. One of the themes of the book is that you will become what you truly believe you will become. If you believe you will be successful and have a happy life, then you will.

There is a great deal of difference between wishing for something and truly believing in it. In order for the Universe to give you what you want, you have to believe you already have it. Then you must project this image each day as if you have already attained it. If you slip back into the "poor me" syndrome, you will also get more of what makes you susceptible to "poor me."

I truly believe we create our experiences throughout our lives, both positive and negative. We may not realize it at the time we are living our creations, but all our potentials were planned by us before we incarnated into this Earth School.

Chapter 4

We Are What We Think We Are

I married my high school sweetheart when I was nineteen years old. We had known each other since we were fifteen, as she lived directly across the alley from me. We dated all through high school, even though I went to public school and she went to Catholic parochial school. I was so twitterpated with her that for a long time I never even recognized the true nature of her beliefs. Barbara often stated to me that she had been born in the wrong place at the wrong time. I realize now that she has some recall of her planning sessions between lives.

We had five wonderful children together over the next nine years, but she always kept repeating to me that she was not supposed to be here, and the kids were not supposed to be born. Most people would have called her mentally ill. After several years of trying to convince her that she WAS here and we DID have the children, I persuaded her to start going to therapy. We went to psychiatrists, psychologists, other kinds of therapists, and the parish priest. Often, at the end of my long work day, after our evening meal and with children tucked away, she would start telling me how hard she had it during the day and the demands that the kids put on her because "she was not supposed to be here and the kids were not either." I would try to help her see the reality, that the children were now part of both our lives and we were all here together on Earth. Sometimes after I got to sleep at night, she would wake me, still trying to convince me of her truth. Neither I nor the professionals were able to crack her obsession.

After about fifteen years of her trauma, I made a change in my career that required us to move to New Richmond, Wisconsin, about three hundred miles away, in the northwestern part of the state. We had purchased a new home there. On the morning we were leaving, with the U-Haul already packed with our belongings, Barbara decided she couldn't move with us. Our children ranged in age from three to fifteen. I was totally shocked and tried to bring her back to the reality of our lives, but she said she had to stay with her "family." I told her that her family was moving and she should come along. She said her "family" was in Milwaukee and she had to stay with them. She had an older brother and younger sister in Milwaukee, but her parents had moved to Florida a few years prior.

So Barbara stayed in Milwaukee, while our five children and I moved to New Richmond. She came up to visit several times, but always had to go back to her roots in Milwaukee. Each time I became more aware of the depth of her belief that she was in the wrong life experience.

On one visit the children told me that she took them for a ride in her car and informed them that she was looking for a railroad crossing where she could park the car and wait for a train to come and kill all of them, as they were not supposed to be here. Needless to say the kids were terrified, and I never allowed her to take them out in a car again.

Because of the felt truth of her beliefs, she was totally unable to enjoy the wonderful potential of this life experience. She missed out on all of the wondrous joys of raising a family of five children. Her recall of her planning sessions before this incarnation was so strong that she could not overcome her deep-seated memories of her original life plan.

I must also point out that her experiences in this incarnation (and everyone else's) are no accident. She, and we, are living one of the potentials that we set up in our planning sessions before we come here. My true belief is that "We are what we think we are." Our free will on this side of the veil allows us to choose one of many potentials that we created before we incarnated into this Earth School.

Chapter 5

What Happens When We Die?

My father moved into my home with Barbara and me about six months after we were married. He had retired at age sixty-three due to health reasons. Dad received Social Security of $130 per month and a pension from Allis-Chalmers of $50 per month. This was not enough for him to live on alone, and he gave the largest part of it to me for room and board. Our property had an upper and lower apartment, each consisting of a kitchen, dining room, living room, full bath, and two bedrooms. We lived in the lower apartment and rented out the upper one for $95 per month. Our payments were only $135 per month, so it was very affordable. Dad lived in one of our bedrooms and Barbara and I shared the other with our new son, Scott. This arrangement worked well for a while, but over the next eight years we had three more children, so our living quarters became very crowded.

I had a good job as a machine operator at the Allen Bradley Company, but became convinced that I should become a life insurance agent about four years after we were married. For the first three years it was touch and go, but then I started making more commissions and got comfortable enough to buy a four-bedroom house on a larger lot in the former town of Grandville, an annexation to Milwaukee.

There are many difficulties, as well as benefits, in having three generations in one household. I know that it was difficult for Dad too because of the constant noise from the kids and because we lived outside of the city, where he could not walk to a store or even a local tavern to have a beer. There came a time when I believed that Dad would be better off in a nursing home for his health and happiness. I also suspected that his constant moans and groans were part of Barbara's problem. I made arrangements with Milwaukee County to assist him in financing the nursing home costs and took him to a rather nice residence on a bluff overlooking Lake Michigan.

I stopped in to visit him the day after we brought him to the residence, but he was not there. I learned that he had walked away right after I dropped him off. It was about two weeks before I tracked him down. He was sharing an apartment with another guy, but was not taking his diabetes medication, so he was hospitalized within a few days. It was late in June and I had planned a camping trip with the family over the July 4 weekend. Dad seemed stable, so I left on the trip after telling him I would see him when I got back.

Upon our return I found that he was in intensive care. They told me that he had a heart problem and I could only visit with him for ten or fifteen minutes. When I went into the ICU, I was surprised to find him sitting up in bed and smiling at me. In the previous several months Dad's speech had been slurred and it was difficult to understand him, but now he was talking clearly and seemed to be very upbeat. We visited for over an hour, and he told me stories of his youth that I had never heard before. When I finally had to leave, I too felt optimistic and felt better about him than I had many months.

I don't know why, but on the way home I started thinking about the various steps I would have to take when he finally did die. When I arrived home, eager to tell Barbara and the kids the good news, Barbara told me that the hospital had called to tell us that Dad had died a few minutes after I left. Did he sense his imminent death? Had he been so happy in the last moments of his life because he knew he was going home?

Mom was a heavy smoker for most of her life. She could not always afford cigarettes, so she bought Bull Durham tobacco and rolled her own. After I left home, we did not get to visit very often because of the 450-mile distance between us. Prior to my first visit back home to see her, right after I turned sixteen, I made a deal with a TV repairman to paint his house (two coats) in exchange for a used black-and-white television set, which I took with me for Mom. She had been able to purchase a forty-acre farm, with buildings, for $4,000. This farm was the love of her life, and she had great pride in the fact that she finally owned a piece of property. The family loved the TV, as they had never had one. I had great joy in giving them something that brought some pleasure into their lives.

At fifty-seven, Mom was diagnosed with lung cancer. This happened around the same time as my career move to northwestern Wisconsin. I was happy to think I would be able to visit her more often and let her get to know my children. But it was not meant to be. Her condition rapidly deteriorated, so I gathered the family for what was to be our last visit. By the time we got there she was bedridden and had difficulty communicating. It was very difficult to go back into the house for what I felt quite sure would be our last farewell. It truly saddens me today that I could not properly say goodbye. I just could not accept that I would not see her again, and I could not talk to her about her pending transition to the other side of the veil.

I have become much more comfortable with this kind of talk. I am now able to discuss their death transition with terminal people, even though it still may be difficult with people that are close to me. From all the reading I have done, I believe the death experience can be totally different for each of us. My understanding is that we all control our death experience by what we believe and what we think will happen. Some people believe they will be greeted by loved ones, or even Jesus, so that is what they will see when they die. Others see themselves as sinners who will be punished with pain and fire, so that is what they will experience. Some people believe they will be attracted to a bright light through a long tunnel, and this too will come about for each as they believe.

Each of us has created our own potentials for our experience in this biology we call our body. We plan this experience during our time between incarnations. Before we incarnate, a curtain is created that bars us from remembering any past-life knowledge. This is done so we can teach or learn in this lifetime. We usually do both.

Just as we do not remember who we really are on the other side of this curtain, we do not remember what death and rebirth are like either. While we live this life we form beliefs and opinions as to who we really are and what we are here for. We are influenced by those individuals and various

19

groups we associate with. We each may have different beliefs because of our religious affiliation, our associations with parents and friends, our workplace, and every other contact we make in this life. Indeed, we are influenced by every experience and thought.

As we move through this life we form our opinions and beliefs of the afterlife (or its absence). By consolidating all of what we learn, over time we form our own story about what will happen when we die.

As our own mind, or inner spirit, actually creates our future, so does it create our death experience. This does not mean that if we think we are going to burn in Hell for eternity that we actually will, but it will cause us to *experience* that pain for a short time after we die, if this be our belief.

We have the ability to make our death whatever we think it to be, but after a short time, whatever we create for ourselves will fade into the wonder and beauty of our true being in the oneness of our Creator. Upon our death, our teacher guides are always there to soothe our transition back to our Higher Self and the true spirit that we really are.

For myself, I have no fear of death, as I believe this is only one of many transitions we make through various incarnations in our past and future. Our bodies are a temporary house for our true spirit, which is eternal.

Just remember, it is what you believe will happen that controls your experience, not what others tell you. You are the creator of all of your own experiences.

You are what you think you are.

Chapter 6

Can You Change Your Beliefs?

Your beliefs are a compilation of all the thoughts and experiences of your life. Consider your mind as a supercomputer. You continually feed in information: each person you meet, every discussion, all of your past beliefs, your reading, each event, other previous life experiences, and the news you hear each day. Then feed in each of your thoughts, memories, or recollections, and your hopes and expectations for the future.

Then, on a continuous basis, your supercomputer sends all of this to a massive central processing unit (CPU) to add to the collection of days stored in your lifetime. We might call this giant CPU "the Universe." Once the CPU has stored and analyzed this information, it responds to you with the outcome of the day's input. If the day has been positive, refreshing, good, uplifting, caring, and loving, that response is going to replicate that input, making you feel good and giving you more of your positive potential for your next day and next week, and so on.

If, however, your day has been negative, downtrodden, a bummer, and it seems that all its events were burdensome and your thoughts were negative, such as *Woe be to me, I have been beaten down again, just like always. I see all the good that is happening to others, but never to me. I always get the bad things. I want good things too, but alas, they must not be for me, as I always seem to get the crappy end of the stick.* If these are your thoughts, then the CPU will analyze them and respond to your day's input with more negativity. Now you have added one more day of downers to the CPU, which will affect all future days.

You can change the output coming from the giant CPU only by

changing the input you give it each day. To change it, you must concentrate, each day, on feeding in information about your proposed change. Each experience, each thought, each desire, each contact you make effects change.

But, you say, *The new day has only given me more bad experiences. My spouse criticized me as soon as I woke up. I burned the pancakes. I missed the 7:45 bus (again) and was late for work. My boss threatened to dock my pay for being tardy. I called one of our best customers and she said she was going to our competitor for her future products. The day just seemed to continue in a negative way, so how can I feed positive information into therea CPU?*

You *can* change the outcome from the Universe, but it is not easy. I might tell you to just change your input and think about positive, happy, rewarding or satisfying experiences to initiate this change. But, you say, *How can I think positive wonderful thoughts when all that happens to me is bad? In other words, how can I think about draining the swamp when I am up to my ass in alligators?*

Well, I did not say it was easy. Any change that we want to be permanent is hard indeed. My advice is to start with something simple that you know you can do. Just start the first day with one thought or one action that you can store away. All of us have at least one good experience each day that we can remember. Just think about that experience for a minute or two and see how that makes you feel. If you do not recall any good experiences, create one! Donate something to a homeless person on your way to work. Now how does that make you feel?

You may say, *I really feel taken advantage of because I think this person is just a lazy beggar and I have enabled her.* But you also could think, *I feel good with my action because I have been able to help provide a breakfast for someone less fortunate than even I am.* You have to remember that you do not control others' actions. You must not judge the actions of others, such as what the homeless person does with your gift. It is your *actions* that the Universe responds to.

When you get to work, really look at those around you and find something you can say to someone that will pick up *their* day: "Your hair really looks nice today" or "Wow, you really have a nice smile." If you look each day for some good thing you can say or do for someone else, you will be able to find it. In order to change the output from the CPU, you must make this a daily habit.

Then, expand on the things you are doing and thinking about so you find yourself spending some minutes each day for do-good, feel-good activities. You will soon learn that the good deeds, thoughts, and actions are contagious and others will start seeing you in a new light. You will begin to find other people actually trying to help you. Yes, YOU!

As you continue to do this, you will be feeding new material into this giant CPU processor (the Universe). Then you will find your life will begin to change for the better. You will find yourself having positive feelings more often. The Universe will start sending you more good opportunities that you may capitalize on for changing your life. You can change your life, but you must visualize that the change has already happened—and live in that change.

Life is like a mirror; you can only get out of it what you put into it.

I want to relate a story to you, the story of a longtime friend; let's call her Fran. Fran is a wonderful, talented person who is extremely bright. She finds it easy to learn and become proficient in anything she sets out to do. She is an accomplished musician and has been able to study and understand some very complex subjects. But Fran has had some very bad experiences in her life that have held her back from enjoying the positive potential she has.

I have known Fran for many years, but in all honesty, she is a "Debbie Downer." I have seldom had conversations with her where she has concentrated only on the positive. No matter what subject I bring up, she seems to find the downside of it. She always relates back to her own bad experiences.

Fran became a recluse, not wanting to communicate with other people in a public setting. She expressed little interest in the people who were around her, even those serving her. You could number those close to her on one hand. Even so, because of her knowledge and her high intellect, she was able to understand and give good advice to others on how they could live more positively, and even change their lives. Those few people that broke the barrier of her defensive posture found her to be a fascinating conversationalist and were eager to follow her suggestions to improve their life.

Unfortunately, she couldn't seem to put her good advice to work for herself. She was always feeding negative information, negative feelings, negative experiences, and negative thoughts into her giant CPU. With her constant bombardment of the Universe with the negative, the Universe gave her back more negative.

I have had many conversations with Fran in recent years, and she has been able to open a new chapter in her life. She has changed many of the negative influences surrounding her daily activities. She now expresses a genuine interest in the people she meets. She has joined several personal improvement groups and has contributed greatly to the members.

She now practices complimenting the people that cross her path each day. She informs her waitresses of their pretty hair or nice smile. She compliments the mechanic who works on her car and befriends the manager of her local grocery store. By practicing some of her own advice, she has made a significant change in her ability to enjoy this lifetime.

We indeed do create our future, just as we have created our past.

Chapter 7

Religion and Spiritual Advancement— Are They the Same?

I have had a great interest in the spiritual element of our existence for many years. While I wasn't raised in any specific religion as a child, I did convert to Catholicism in my mid-teens, as my then-girlfriend and her family influenced me and encouraged me to learn their beliefs. While I got quite involved with the church early on, even becoming the president of the Holy Name Society, I always had questions for the priest. One involved the biblical explanation of creation. God created Adam and Eve as the first people, and they had children, including Cain and Abel. The Bible says when Cain came of age he was sent off into the wilderness to find a wife. How did he find a wife in the wilderness when his family was the first family created by God? Another question involved the directive that wives should be submissive to their husbands. This has led many to believe that the male (husband) is better than the female (wife). Am I supposed to believe that I am superior to my spouse? Am I smarter and stronger, or do I have greater knowledge than she does?

In real life I have learned that many female spouses have the ability to manipulate and control most of the decisions made by a married couple. For the male readers here—now be honest—do you feel in control of your marriage to the point of telling your wife what color the living room is going to be painted? If so, I'll bet you don't get your way in other challenges in your day-to-day relationship.

While I had many discussions with the priest and got lots of information, I seldom got satisfactory explanations to many of my questions. When he finally came down to an answer, it would often be, "Some things you just have to believe with a grain of faith."

Among many significant changes in my youth, I drifted from the Catholic Church to the United Methodists, and I studied with the Jehovah's Witnesses for several years. All of the organized religions wanted me to believe that the Bible is "The Word of God" and is to be taken quite literally. It seems to me that anyone can prove any point, pro or con, by using their own interpretation of scripture. In my real life experience, I have found that the Bible thumpers have been the ones with the least scruples when dealing with others. I have had several business dealings over the years with men who carry their Bible with them (for show), but I found in my dealings with them that they were totally in it for themselves with little or no regard for those that they did business with.

I want to emphasize here that my experiences have been within the framework of the Christian religion, which is just one of the many religions in existence today. I am in no way totally negative on what religion does for many people. I have some very good friends with strong religious beliefs who are wonderful people. Many are charitable and honest and truly believe in the very positive aspects of their faith. If I have a beef with organized religion, it is with the leadership of these organizations. It is my opinion that the (usually) male leaders of these churches get into power by adjusting their interpretations of scripture to place and keep themselves in power. Along the way, unfortunately, they belittle women to a point where they are not allowed to be religious leaders and are told to be subservient to men. Many times these leaders will defy science, and even reason, if it promotes their views to do so.

Let me assure you, I do believe in the God Source. I believe that you should love your fellow humans as you love God, and as you love yourself. We should not limit "Love your neighbor as yourself" by color, nationality, or religious belief.

But many humans have attained leadership positions by using religion as a way to control others. Once they have this control, they can infuse hate, greed, and fear as tools to cause disagreement and even wars, all to further their own power. These beliefs include love of country, loyalty to the flag, and the belief that we are better or more pure of heart and mind then the "others." These leaders create thoughts like, "If we don't take them, they will take us." Like sheep, we then follow them by trying to impose our beliefs on "the enemy" (or die trying).

The people that we hold as the enemy are the same as we are. They are creations of the same God. They have loves and desires just as we do. They do not want to go off to war or send their young children off to war. The only hate they have for us has been imposed by *their* leaders, political or religious. Such leaders have almost always been at the source of world conflict. Some of these leaders have a strong belief that their religion is the only way to heaven. Many have missionaries that travel all over the world to try to impose their beliefs on others. They often call these others "heathens" and do their best to influence them by disparaging their "heathen beliefs" in favor of their own. While this missionary work has been done in countries all over the world, let's take our own American Indians as an example.

Native Americans have always believed in God. They believe that God is in everything. They believe in the spirits of the buffalo, the trees, the crops, the eagle, and so on. The European missionaries did not believe in this interpretation of the God Source. The missionaries called this belief heathenistic. They did their best to either convert the Indians or wipe out their beliefs. As it turns out, the Native Americans were probably closer to the truth than the missionaries who condemned them. As we know now, everything is made up of the vibrating energy of the God Source. The trees, the buffalo, the eagle, and yes, even our bodies are made up of this vibrating energy that is from the God Source. Think of how different this nation might be if the Europeans had come to this continent with love and acceptance rather than with conquest as their goal.

Love thy neighbor as thyself is written in the basic scriptures of almost every religion in the world. The problem is, our religious leaders try to tell us who "our neighbors" are. *Certainly*, they say, *our neighbors do not include people of other beliefs and religions. They don't think like us. They must be less than us.* Don't you believe this! Not for a second! The neighbors that the scriptures refer to are all the people of the world. Our neighbors include all nationalities, all races, and all humans. In loving our neighbors as ourselves, think about it. If we do not love ourselves, how can we be effective in loving our neighbors?

So what does it mean to "love ourselves"? I believe there are many steps involved in loving ourselves. We must, first of all, be willing to forgive ourselves for our self-judged misdeeds. If we carry around this guilt all the time, it will hamper our ability to forgive others.

We must also take care of, and respect, the biological bodies that are hosting us in this incarnation. If we abuse our own bodies, we then find it easier to accept the abuse of others.

We must not, however, put ourselves above others nor envy others, as we are all angels of God. Even Jesus called us "my brothers and sisters." When we learn to love our neighbors as ourselves, we will have peace.

I am not sure who should receive credit to for the following quote, and even Google doesn't know for sure (maybe Jimi Hendrix?), but I think it is an appropriate one with which to close this chapter.

When the power of love overcomes the love of power, the world will have peace.

Chapter 8

Be Careful What You Think About

I am a believer in reincarnation. I believe we reincarnate many times in our process of evolving. Our Higher Self, or spirit being, creates these experiences for growth, a process of our evolvement. There are only two reasons we reincarnate. One is to learn and evolve, the other is to teach and help others to evolve. In any single lifetime, we always do both.

We learn in many different capacities. We learn what we dislike or like. We learn what is good and what is bad, and what is right or wrong. Are you noticing a pattern here? Each lesson gives us a choice. We have free will in each of the choices we make. Each day in our lives we have choices to make. The choice to be good or bad, happy or sad, generous or greedy, loving or hateful, successful or failing; I could go on and on, but you get the point.

Each decision we make is part of our personal evolvement. Notice I did not say each *good* decision; *each* decision is a contribution to the process. In this process we are constantly creating ourselves and thus, evolving. What we actually become, then, is a compilation of each and every thought and deed and decision we have made (or not) over our lifetime or combination of lifetimes.

Each of us is at a different stage of evolving. As an example, Mother Teresa has evolved to a different level than Hitler. All of us, even Mother Teresa, have made some less-than-positive decisions from time to time. This is not a bad thing, as these lessons are used to better ourselves and others.

We also influence others with each of these daily decisions. Thus we accomplish the second purpose of our existence: to teach. We are continually observed by others, and they learn from us and our experiences, just as we learn from them and their experiences. We should not look back at any of our decisions as negative if we, or someone else, have learned from the experience.

I have sometimes pondered over why a baby may be born and live for only a short time before passing again. My conclusion is that this life spirit came over to teach more than to learn. The lessons they give may be to help us see how we and others react with love, sadness, or empathy to a generous spirit that gave of itself through the creation process.

Just as we are evolving in each of our lifetimes, so too does the mass consciousness evolve. Each individual is a part of the whole and contributes to what the whole is. Each decision any individual makes contributes on a daily basis to what the whole entity learns. For the moment, let's call this whole entity "the human race," even though it is much larger than that.

If the majority of this entity expresses hate and vengeance, then that is how the human race evolves. If, however, the majority expresses love and peace, then that is what creates the ever-evolving human race. If you think you don't, or can't, make a difference, then you are not correct. Each decision we make, even each thought we have, every minute, contributes to the mass consciousness. Let us call this mass consciousness "the world as we know it."

If we are constantly thinking and talking about negative or bad things, then that is what the world becomes. Even if our thought is only something like *War and hate are bad*, it still contributes to the overall negative input. Our thoughts and actions must be positive and profess love and peace. We should think about all the good things that we can do and that can be done by others.

The thoughts and deeds, even from one soul, change the world.

One of the most generous souls the world has ever known was Mother Teresa. When asked if she would participate in a march against war, she refused. However, when asked to participate in a peace rally, she readily accepted.

We must be careful of the very words we use to express our thoughts.

As the Universe hears the words of you, and of others, it is very generous in returning to us more of what it hears and sees. You must also remember that your thoughts control only your destiny. You do not control other individuals. Each soul controls its own destiny. Mind you, I am not saying that your thoughts do not influence those around you, but everyone has free will.

Let's use an example that history is familiar with. Was it not said that Hitler controlled the masses? First, we must understand that as human beings, we have a natural dislike for confrontation. Many times we will find it easier to "go along" with something just to avoid conflict. We must also remember that we are influenced by what is happening around us each day. I am sure that if the young Hitler in leadership had said "Let's kill millions of people," he would not have received a good reception. He did things very gradually, and while people may not have approved, it was easier to go along than to face a confrontation. After months and years of propaganda, people begin to believe and follow. Hitler also used the element of fear to make people stay in line. They knew that their very neighbors could report them, and they could be eliminated. We must always be aware of the leadership we follow.

Let's use another example, that of drug addiction. Most drug addicts do not believe they have a problem. They feel that they are "in control" and can stop using at any time. I know this because my daughter Lisa is a self-admitted drug addict. Unbeknownst to us at the time, Lisa started experimenting with drugs when she was fourteen years old. She wanted to fit in with her friends, even though she knew it was wrong. As things progressed, she got more and more hooked.

I think we can all remember when we were teenagers and the thrill we got through doing something that we knew our parents wouldn't approve of. (Maybe that isn't all bad; perhaps if we do not create a rift of sorts, our parents will never want us to leave home.) During those years, our bodies look more adult than child, but our adult mental capacity is still to be learned. Our bodies grow without thought or plan, but our minds have to be trained. We are heavily influenced by our need to be accepted by our peer group, and we even do things we know are wrong to obtain that acceptance. That is how Lisa started her drug habit. For us, it seemed like she just flipped a switch and was transformed from a wonderful, smiling, affectionate girl to a surly, uncooperative, and disobedient stranger. We attributed this attitude to her being a teenager and never even thought of her being on drugs. After all, she was the youngest of six siblings, and none of them used drugs.

Lisa started skipping school and we started getting truancy calls. It got to a point where we would drive her to school and watch her go in the building, and she would just walk through the school and out another door. The need for drugs completely overtook her. She started running away and staying with her drug-using friends. We would frantically try to track her down and bring her home, again and again. She knew that she should quit drugs, but even when she would try, the thrill and pleasure she got from using pulled her back. She went through rehab and stopped using for eight years. During that time she got married and give us two very wonderful granddaughters. But the draw of drugs is very powerful and she relapsed. This contributed to a divorce and shared custody of her daughters.

Lisa worked very hard on quitting once more, and this time she hoped for the strength to stop for good. She married a second time and stayed clean during her third pregnancy, providing us with an adorable grandson. Alas, the habit called again, with more severe results than ever. She lost custody of her children and experienced great sadness and feelings of degradation.

Like Hitler's mind control of the German populace, the drug habit starts with a casual acceptance of what is a seemingly a small bad act. Drug addicts never start out with the goal of becoming totally drug dependent. It just happens as small indiscretions get repeated over time.

Lisa now has a habit that is very difficult to change. We always seem to have logical justifications for our actions, good or bad, at the time we do them. There is always an excuse for the drug addict to relapse, but the real reason is that they see themselves as a drug addict. Even Alcoholics Anonymous still has participants repeat at each meeting: "I am an alcoholic." Remember, "We become what we think." If we constantly tell the Universe that we are an addict, the Universe reinforces our belief: "Yes, I am an addict." Instead, we have to tell the Universe that we are a *recovered* addict. The change in wording may seem small, but the message is very different. If we truly consider ourselves recovered, then we will be.

We love Lisa dearly and will always be there for her, but her permanent recovery will come only when she truly believes she is recovered and professes it to the Universe. While it is difficult for us, we must remember that we do not control other people's lives. Just our own.

Chapter 9

Can We Create the Perfect World?

We, as a whole, have created a world where all of our emotions can be experienced. We see around us evidence of these emotional experiences every day. Love, hate, comfort, suffering, pleasant and unpleasant smells and sounds—these are but few of the items we witness daily. Some of the experiences we choose give us the feelings we desire. Many of these experiences require the participation and, at best, the cooperation of other people to get the ultimate satisfaction desired.

Here is where the rub comes in. Other people may not have the same desires and goals as ourselves. This can create a less-than-satisfactory outcome. Sex and love are examples where this can occur. It may be possible that the participants have a different desired outcome, causing disappointment for one or all of them.

The desire to be dominant or to be the best in any contest (games, sports, politics, or war) creates winners and losers with, many times, very traumatic outcomes. Are we now creating mechanisms to take care of all of the inner desires we wish to experience without affecting other entities?

Welcome to the cyber world! This is a place where we can, indeed, experience satisfaction of almost any desire we can dream up. We can compete in sports without pain. We can kill our enemies without paying a penalty. We can have relationships without worry of rejection. We can be totally absorbed in whatever we choose without affecting others.

Does this not sound like the cyber world we have created?

I used to believe that the violent games our kids were playing on their laptops or handhelds was causing them to grow up to be violent to others. While this still may be a fact, I think there may be another side to it. Maybe we all have a potential for violence, which can be acted out. Is it not possible that by acting this out on the computer, we need not act it out in our physical world?

One of the things we experience in our physical world that we do not in either the cyber world or spiritual world is physical pain. We could also say that physical pleasure may not be obtained in the cyber world. While this may be true, are not both sensations created by our thoughts? Can we not create any desired results strictly in our minds?

Creating the "perfect world" is within our grasp, but we must concentrate on the word "create." We, as individual spirits, can create anything we desire.

Yes, I said anything.

We chose to come to this "Earth School" at this particular time in history so we could experience what is going on around us right now. We are learning from this experience as we are creating an example for others to learn from. Some of us may take a passive role in this Earth School and choose not to create change. Others may be very active in creating violence, or the love of peace, or any other of an infinite number of potential creations.

It is easy to love the peacemaker. We must also love the souls that have chosen violence in this incarnation. They are wonderful spirits on the other side of the veil, just as we are. They chose their role in this Earth School so as to teach. Do we not learn lessons from war and violence, even if it is also true that we despise it?

In order to create the "perfect world," we must understand what is imperfect. And we must also understand that perfection may be different for different people. Is your "perfect world" the same as mine? Do you begin to see the extreme difficulty in coming up with this "perfect world"?

As we evolve on a spiritual level, we enjoy each of these steps of the evolutionary process. To evolve, we must see all of the aspects of our physical world just to have this experience. Would a school that taught only the very positive aspects of this physical life prepare us for the real world?

In between lives we chose this particular time in history to reincarnate so we could experience all that surrounds us right now. Are we learning what we came here to learn? I hope so. Each of us can learn from our experiences in this Earth School.

If we want perfection, we must return to our spiritual home. If we had perfection in this Earth School, there would be no reason to incarnate to it.

We can create the perfect world, and maybe we will, but not in this lesson.

Chapter 10

Time, or Progress, as the Unit of Evolvement?

I have had a hard time understanding that on the other side of the veil there is no such thing as time. It has been explained that time is like a toy train running on a circular track, so in reality there is no beginning and no end to it. We can get on the train at any point in its route. Thus, if we wanted to come into one of our incarnations in the pioneer days, or even as a soldier in the Roman army, we can choose that experience. We can enter this Earth School at any point in history that allows us to teach or learn the lessons required for ourselves or our *soul group* (more on this concept later) to progress.

While on this side of the veil we experience time, and measure time, in many ways, but because we can come into this time frame at any entry point in the past or in the future, time is not relevant on the other side, where all time is available to us. All time is going on simultaneously, and we can choose the time frame we wish to experience (anyplace on the train tracks).

If this be fact, then what unit of measurement might be used on the other side of the veil?

I wonder if we could think about "progress," of our soul and soul group, as that unit of measurement? Our soul continues to evolve with each experience. Mind you, that means each thought that we have ever had. Because each soul is eternal, there is no final goal or end to this progress. All souls are at different stages of development and seeking different experiences in this Earth School for their own evolvement. When we talk about "old souls," we are not using a time measurement but rather measuring the evolvement of that soul's experience.

One true measure of a person's evolution is their ability to turn a negative into a positive. To dwell on the negative and use judgment or fear-based thought does not feed the truth. The concern should always be how to make the most positive use of one's time in this school, whether that time is spent in a wheelchair or running marathons.

We create our own potentials for this Earth lifetime while we are in between lives. While in this Earth life we then have free will to accept these potentials—or not. Whatever potentials we choose to ignore will be carried forward as future potentials. We should not live in fear of failing to accept the potentials that we set up for ourselves or our soul group, as we are loved, unconditionally, on the other side of the veil.

It could be said that Hitler influenced more souls than Mother Teresa. We must remember that a negative influence can affect people in a positive way. We should not condemn our neighbor for teaching us, even if the lesson is negative. That generous soul reincarnated as a teacher and is truly loved on the other side of the veil.

Chapter 11

If There Is Good, Must We Have Bad?

While some of us have acquired great monetary rewards in this lifetime, others are monetarily poor. Some souls created the experience of great love for the whole of this Earth School, while others may be the subjects of hate and fear or greed. Each of us has created our own potentials. Each of us also has the free-will choice to pick and choose which of these potentials we will follow. Each of these chosen experiences helps the overall God spirit in the evolutionary process.

You may question why the negatives are necessary, but stop and think about it. Without the knowledge of bad, how would we know what is good? Is this not a learning experience for all, being good or bad?

The Christian Bible tells the story of Adam and Eve in the Garden of Eden. All in the garden was good. Adam and Eve originally had no knowledge of good or bad because they did not have any understanding of what bad was. In order to evolve, our God entity needs to investigate and understand everything that is possible. Thus, Adam and Eve, just as you and I, had this desire to see more, do more, experience more, and become more. If anything is possible, our curiosity requires that we investigate the possibility.

Adam and Eve had to leave the garden of perfection before they could begin to understand what perfection was. We, as descendants of this biological experiment of the God Source, have that same need, the need to understand All That Is. Each of us, in this incarnation, can cite examples of where some good has come from a bad experience, or vice versa. The following examples are recollections from my lessons that are close to my heart.

Example One: I knew a couple of twenty-somethings who were quite aloof, and both were far from being extroverts. I was not close enough to them to know what their personal relationship was like, but their public personas seemed to say "Leave us alone." I was pleased to hear that this couple was bringing a new life into this Earth School. As we know, this always brings great change into our lives. Most often the long-term change it brings is for the better. On the day the baby was born, I received the bad news that she had been born with a severe internal malfunction. The doctors said there was nothing that could be done and gave the baby's life expectancy in hours, not days. I went to the hospital to visit the parents and to wish the newborn well on her short journey. I found a scene I did not expect. I was not allowed to go into the room where the baby was, but could see her through the window. I saw both of her parents there holding the newborn, nuzzling her, and loving her.

While she did not survive for even two full days, you could see the love she brought into her parents' relationship. In addition, the newborn had many visitors who brought love and empathy for the parents. The parents realized that there were many people they could consider friends. Even the friends were visiting with each other and became closer because of the experience.

That little soul came into this world for only a few hours but brought more love and affection into the lives of those around her than some people see in a much longer lifetime. We have much to be thankful for this generous spirit that gave so many of us an unforgettable experience.

Example Two: Many times I find it difficult to understand my daughter's drug addiction. It seems, at times, that my entire goal is to try and change her, to help her become "normal." If I could only look at this from the forty-thousand-foot level, maybe I could see some of the good her generous soul is creating. She is giving up so many potentials in this life that she could enjoy, but she is also creating an experience for those of us that are close to her to learn from.

Her children have lost her as a mother, in our image of what motherhood is, but they have seen firsthand the harm that drugs do when used inappropriately. They have an example, each day, of what not to do. This example goes even deeper in that her children can spread the message of inappropriate drug use to their friends. In a broader perspective, our twelve grandchildren also see this example and very hopefully will avoid having the same problems.

Is this but another example of using a bad experience to create good? My daughter may well be saving many souls from the terrible experience of drug addiction by taking on this potential that she created. My love for her is only enhanced by knowing that there is a very convincing reason that she took this difficult route in her current incarnation so as to potentially help others.

In both examples a soul incarnated to help other souls along their route of evolving. I believe one of the challenges each of us have is to observe both the good and the bad things around us and learn from them, rather than choosing to condemn them. If we live each day as if it were our last, we will be much more generous to ourselves and others.

Chapter 12

Quantum Physics (Oh, No!) An Explanation of Creation?

I think there is a general perception that quantum physics is this very complex science that requires being a geek's geek to begin to understand its concepts. My conversation on this topic will not be anything near that level. My sister, Jan, got me interested in the basic concepts many years ago. The subject fascinated me to a point that I studied and tried to absorb the scientific principles. The more I got into it, the more interested I became. Now understand that if I were tested on the scientific details of quantum physics, I would probably fail miserably. What has fascinated me about the science has been the ability to use this knowledge as a basis of understanding some of the realities of life. But wait, I will get into that later.

Okay, here goes! In my own words. Quantum physics is the study of breaking down all matter into its very smallest components. We can start with any physical object; let's say that chair you're sitting on. We can start by determining the basic elements making up its wood, steel, and fabric. Then we break these elements down into molecules. Then we further break the molecules down into atoms, then protons, electrons, and even photons. Science has now proven that all matter, in its smallest components, is made up of pure vibrating energy. Think about this: science is telling us is that everything is made up of nothing. Well, nothing but vibrating energy. Do WE then create the solidness?

Now I am sure that any educated scientist will laugh at my simplistic explanation. I have glossed over most of the aspects of the science, but that is not as important as the things that we can now understand because of the science. If everything is made up of vibrating energy, then what is the source of all of this energy? What causes some of this energy to make up elements that in turn make up "things"?

Here is where I may lose some of you, but let's go.

Is it possible that this vibrating energy is coming from the God Source? (Ask yourself: where else would it come from?) If this be fact, then everything that is, is created by the God Source. It is THE source that creates "all things" that come into existence.

That chair you are sitting in, then, was created by the God Source . . .

But, you say, why would God have created this chair? For the answer, let's go one step deeper. Remember, everything is made up of vibrating energy. This means that you and I are made up of vibrating energy, just like the chair. Well, that's what science tells us.

Let me now tell you a story. A story about possibilities. A story for you to enjoy. A story that you may think is possible, or not.

In the beginning God created the heavens and the Earth. (Here we go again.) Now God, as the source of vibrating energy, can create anything It wants to. So let's start with the big things. First, God created a limitless supply of universes with millions of stars, planets, and moons in all of these universes. God was pleased with Its creations.

Then God created life forms from these elements to enjoy the happenings of life itself. She/He created the plants and animals and was amused by these creations.

God then decided that, to enjoy all of the aspects of life, It had to provide partners to share and enjoy these creations. God then created spirit, which we may call our soul, or our Higher Self. God was further pleased with the creation of spirits, and all were in agreement at the wonder and beauty of these creations.

But spirit had no biology so as to experience the aspects of physical life. Being a higher part of the God Source, spirit also had the power to create. Spirit decided that to evolve more fully, It should set up this school of learning where free will could be experienced, without the knowledge of perfection. In this Earth School, Homo sapiens was the most evolved form of life, so spirit entered these biological forms. Voila—humans.

Spirit purposely limited the knowledge of perfection so as to see how life might evolve without the total understanding of creation. Spirit wanted to protect these creations, so She/He created a garden where no harm could come to the new life form. This garden protected from the knowledge of good versus bad, and the evolutionary process quickly decided that this new biology should have free will when incarnated. Thus the human race evolved from these elements and the spirit's unlimited appetite for knowledge: the knowledge of choice and knowing good from bad.

When spirit created this new entity, partly spirit and partly biology, its full knowledge had to be limited so as to allow free choice; free choice allowed natural evolution without the knowledge of perfection. But the question was, and still is, will this new human evolve toward perfection, or something else?

Thus, this Earth School continues.

Chapter 13

Why Are We Here, Now?

Over the years in this incarnation, I have had many opportunities and much experience in learning and trying to understand why I am here. While you may agree, or not, I am sharing some of the conclusions I have arrived at.

As part of our original God spirit, all spirits are an extension of God. Each spirit has all the powers of the God spirit because they are part of the whole of All That Is. All spirits have the power, and yes, the duty, to create.

We, as humans, are also part of spirit. We too have a duty to create.

We, as human entities in this Earth School, do not look at ourselves as being able to actually create anything. The reason for this is that for this Earth School to work, the memories of our true powers, our true higher selves, have been shielded with a temporary curtain. For some this is a very heavy curtain that allows no light to pass. Without the light, these individuals have little guidance as to their direction. For others the curtain allows some light to pass, giving them more memory of the perfection of the other side. And for still others, this curtain is very sheer, allowing more recall of who they are and why they are in this school.

We are all a part of a soul group that continues to evolve. This soul group may reincarnate over many lifetimes to help each member accomplish their individual goals in evolution. In between lives we are counseled as to the lessons we should learn and the best place to go to create the environment to realize these goals. This may be the Earth School, or it could be anywhere in the multiple universes that creates the best circumstances for learning our particular lesson.

Once we have picked out our desired lesson, we create the potentials for our life experience with our soul group. If this lesson is best served with the use of free will, we may end up in this Earth School. When we are planning our Earth School test of free will, we set up a lifetime of potentials. Each experience we plan may, or may not, occur. The test with our free will is this: Which way will we go? Will we learn our lesson as planned, or will we be distracted by other available alternatives?

Our soul group is very active in this planning process. Who will be our parents, our friends, our spouse, or our children? What part will each of these play in our overall lesson? How will other souls be affected by the decisions we make? Who, among our soul group, may benefit from being a part of this lesson?

We then determine the time in history that may be best for our particular lesson. This could be the Dark Ages, or the time that Jesus taught, or our current times. There are an infinite number of possible choices and places within the past or the future.

We also determine what race we will be, what religion we will we be influenced by, and in what part of the world we will live. All of this will affect the lessons we learn and the teaching we give.

Once we complete a lifetime (it may be short or long), we return home to the other side of the curtain. We again meet with our counselors to review and determine how far we have come with our lessons. Then we determine our next steps in the never-ending evolutionary process. Amen. We start anew.

Another reason we reincarnate as a part of a soul group is to teach. If we are a teacher, we play our part in this biology to help others with their lessons. This may be accomplished in many different ways. As a teacher we may be a leader, a mentor, or even a victim for our charges to learn their lesson.

By being a victim, we may serve as a teacher for many souls. Let me give an example. I could never understand why a soul would reincarnate to suffer a terrible disease or be molested or even murdered as a child by another soul. The purpose may be to teach those other souls in their soul group about compassion, or sense of loss at the child's demise. This same experience may teach others about the need to provide support and love for those souls closest to the deceased.

You might ask, what loving soul could possibly come into a life with the potential of being a molester or a murderer? We must remember that the whole experience of teaching this lesson to many souls could not happen if the offense were not committed. Spirit needs all potential experience to evolve.

We must understand that all souls are loved and no soul is inherently bad, but only performs their part in the lessons as the potentials were set up.

How could we understand what is good without knowing what is bad?

Chapter 14

Soul Interference

Each of us, as souls, has created this experience in the Earth School. Our soulmates planned this lifetime with us so as to help us accomplish our lessons. We must think about the fact that even though the other soulmates reincarnated to help us with our evolution, they too have lessons in this incarnation.

We often feel that we should be more involved with decisions for the people around us, particularly those closest to us. We have all witnessed the person who feels that he or she is in control of everything, including us and everyone around us. While this experience of control may be part of their lesson, it also may be imposing limitations on our, and others', lessons. We chose to have that controlling person as a part of our experience, just as they chose to have the controlling tendencies in their personality.

We must not forget that we have free choice. We may remove ourselves from any situation that we feel, in our hearts, is not right for us.

If we happen to be the controller, we must remember that we do not control other souls. As the controller, we may have been chosen by another soul to be just that, their controller. We must also remember that the souls around us do not have to conform to our standards. They have their own goals, which could be very different from what we think is right for them. We do not have to approve of what they do.

These words are easy to say, but in real life may be hard to follow. I have been a controller, to a great extent, in this incarnation. I have tried to impose my standards on those close to me. For example, I devoted a great deal of my life to my career. My average work week was over sixty hours.

I started early and worked late into the evening, even working Saturdays and sometimes Sundays if I had a project to complete. I, too often, put my work ahead of my family and friends. While this was good for my career, it caused me to miss out on a lot of the non-business life going on around me. I often missed my kids' sports or performance events and did not show empathy with the trials and tribulations of my family, friends, or employees.

While I hired many wonderful employees over the years, I could never figure out why they did not have the same work standards as I did. It always seemed to me that I wanted their success more than they did. It is only in later life that I have begun to understand that they had their own goals in this life. Their goals may very well have been different from mine. I have definitely tried to impose my standards on everyone around me. Is this a natural tendency? Do you try to do the same thing? Be honest now as you think about it.

We must try to remember that we do not control other souls' incarnations. We should not be disappointed when others don't live up to our expectations. We must remember that all souls write their own play for this incarnation. Even though they made us the part of that play, it is their lesson that is important to them.

Chapter 15

The Power and Limitations of Our Mind

I have had an interest in learning more about the power of the mind for many years. I have read many books on the subject and continue to eagerly learn. At one point I was asked to give a speech on the subject. I would like to reproduce this speech here. The title was "The Power and Limitations of Our Mind."

We are told that we use only a small percentage of the power of our brain. Is this because we have set our own limitations on what we think we can do? Do we lose our potential in any endeavor because we put up walls or limits on ourselves? I want to talk with you today about the amazing, powerful, and untapped potential each and every one of us possess to obtain and achieve our heart's desires.

We have many powers as infants and young children because we do not realize that we have limits, albeit our own learned limits. As a very young child we have an almost unlimited learning capacity. As we grow we are told of our limits. For example, we are told, "you don't really have an imaginary friend and if you keep talking about it you will be punished." Another example might be "Johnny is too young to be trained or educated. Let the kid be a kid and play, watch TV, or any other less productive activity." We are trained very young that we have limits on what we can do.

The Bible says that if we had the faith of but the size of a grain of mustard seed we can move mountains. Do we believe that, or do we say that this is just a story? It has nothing to do with reality. What you believe is what will come about for you.

In our youth we are constantly bombarded with all of the things we cannot do. Many of these things are done to keep us safe or protect us from predators. "Do not talk with strangers. Do not cross the street. Stay in your boundaries." We are constantly given limits on what we can do and even how we can think. "There is no such thing as ghosts." "You are too young to learn about that." These are just a few examples of our learned limits.

Back in the 1800s there was a common belief that if the human body were to move faster than 25 mph you would bleed from your eyes and ears and other orifices. Of course, the automobile proved this belief to be wrong.

For many years everyone knew that it was impossible for a human to run fast enough to break the four-minute mile. This was another barrier that served to hold us back. Roger Bannister broke that barrier and others almost immediately followed.

Until 1492 people thought the Earth was flat. Columbus and his brave crew set sail to prove this wrong. As we know now, his voyage did not prove the Earth was round, because he only sailed halfway around the globe. The most important accomplishment of his voyage was that he got people to believe the world was round. In the process he found a new land and new people the Europeans never knew about. (I will not go into the fact that Columbus was not the first to discover the American continents.)

As we are breaking many of these self-imposed or society-imposed barriers, we are expanding the horizons of our physical and mental capacities. We must, however, learn to expand the use of our mind power in the same manner. We must learn to think "outside the box."

Let me tell you a story. A story about a fish named Goldie.

Goldie was a very normal fish. She lived in a pond that made a very comfortable home for her and all of her fish relatives. She spent her days doing what all fish do. She played with her friends, foraged for food. And was always on the lookout for predators who would look at her as food. Goldie knew her pond very well.

She knew the other fish, the plants, the rocks, and each nook and cranny of her pond. This was her world and she was happy with it. This was Goldie's world.

One day as Goldie was foraging for food she came upon an unexpected treat. There on the floor of her pond was a large and delicious-looking worm. Goldie could hardly believe her good fortune of finding such a satisfying morsel and she quickly sucked it into her mouth. This was one action that would change Goldie's life forever.

Suddenly she felt a searing pain in her mouth as she was pulled up toward the top of her world at such a speed that she knew she would bump the sky. Imagine her surprise when she actually went right through the top of her world into a new world.

Goldie saw many strange new things in this new world. She saw large trees and grasses and animals that she never imagined existed. The main new experience was being grabbed by this monster while the source of the pain was removed.

Then she felt the monster remove the grip and felt herself falling through this new world, and like magic, she was back in her pond.

Just think about Goldie's excitement to tell all her friends of this new experience, this new world. She told of the trees and animals and the light in the great new sky. She talked of the monsters that grabbed her and told of all her new experiences. Her friends seem to listen with interest; however, they soon realized that Goldie had "lost her grip." "She had gone off the deep end." Yes, they concluded that Goldie was CRAZY.

All the leader fish in the pond made the decision to banish Goldie to the part of the pond reserved for the "crazies." They didn't want Goldie's sickness to spread to the other fish in the pond. They all knew that there was only one world.

Being banished from the group was a very lonely experience. No longer could she play with her friends or learn the "normal" things from her teachers.

Goldie just knew that this experience really happened and that she wasn't crazy. She began to formulate a plan to prove that her experience was real. She knew that the ceiling, or sky, of her world was how she got into the new world. If she could only get through the ceiling again she might be in this other world.

She decided to try to break through the ceiling. She would start at one end of the pond and swim as fast as she could to the other end and as she reached the far side, crash into the ceiling. And she did. She swam across the pond at a speed she had never swum before. As she reached the far end she crashed into the ceiling and, to her great satisfaction, she found herself transferring worlds again. As she entered this new world, now for the second time, she flopped up in some rocks and again observed the strange phenomena of the new world. It proved that this was not a comfortable place to be as she quickly found she could not absorb oxygen through her gills. She flopped a couple of times right into a stream that she had never realized was there. Another new world for her. This was much more comfortable, as she could breathe easy.

Goldie began to swim around her new world and discovered many new things. As she swam down the stream she soon found herself in another pond very similar to the one she grew up in. She met a new school of fish that were very curious about her. They wanted to know where she came from and how she got there.

Goldie proceeded to tell them of the other worlds she had been in and how she was able to escape from one world to another. The other fish in the pond listened to her with great interest and reverence. They quickly started calling her "the wise one." They bowed before her and respected her because she came from another world.

In this new world she became a revered leader. She was the only fish in the pond that had seen different worlds. Even now, Goldie has a problem trying to understand why talking of her experiences in one pond ended up landing her in the loony bin while in the other pond the fish made her a leader.

Is there a simile between Goldie and ourselves in that we only believe what our senses can find? Do we, like the fish in the pond, not believe there can be another world? Do we believe only what we had been trained to learn, or might we have an open mind to accept new ideas? Can we accept the fact that some of these ideas may be in conflict with what society has taught us?

As our mass consciousness develops we learn things from our social groups, or even humankind as a whole. The way we found out that the human body could exceed the 25 mph limit was by having someone test that limit. There was someone that was able to step "outside the box" and proved that there was no such limit.

We set our limits by our beliefs in what we can do. Can our minds move mountains? No, we say. Can we travel without our bodies? No, we say. Can we cause physical reality to change with only our thoughts? No, we say. Can we be successful in our lives? Yes, but only within the limits we set for ourselves, we say. Can we increase our income? Yes, but only with the same self-imposed limitations. How many of these learned perceptions have held us back from our true potential?

We use only a small portion of the power of our mind because that is all we believe we can use. We do have an unlimited source of energy to draw on (the God Source). We must learn how to use this energy. We must begin to believe in the power of our mind.

Each of us will be as successful as we truly believe we will be! Don't allow yourself to be limited by self-imposed, or society-imposed, limitations.

The U.S. Army had a slogan that said "Be all that you can be; join the Army."

I do not believe you have to join the Army, or anything else, to be all that you can be. You just have to BELIEVE, inside yourself, that you already are that belief, and it will come about.

Don't limit your future by self-imposed beliefs. You can make your future anything you want it to be. It is within your power alone to create your future experiences.

Chapter 16

What You Believe Will Be, Will Be

Many inventions exist to help us along our path, but I believe the computer was developed to help us begin to realize the unlimited power each of us has in our mind. I believe we are in the process of a quantum leap in the use of this brainpower. I bought the first computer for my office in the late 70s. Back then we talked about memory capacity in kilobytes. Later on we went to megabytes, gigabytes, and petabytes, and now we really believe as a population that computers can only get smaller, work faster, and hold more information. Sixty years ago computers were the size of your bedroom and held less information than some wristwatches have today. Our minds have grown to accept rapid expansion as it relates to technology in the past few years.

Now, let's think about that computer within each of us: our brain. Our brain has more computation power than the largest computer ever built. The computer can do calculations at very rapid rates, but it cannot reason. It cannot know what is morally right or wrong in any given situation. The computer cannot think its way through a problem beyond its programmed capabilities. It can only do things the way it has been programmed. (Even this perception is evolving, however.)

Our brain has an unlimited amount of potential energy that can be transferred through our thoughts to whatever we want to do. It has been said that in each minor decision we make, our brain calculates many alternatives and comes up with the best decision for that instant. Our brain is capable of doing so much more than what we consciously use it for.

Some people can communicate telepathically and instantly with others who are emotionally close to them, even at a great physical distance. I think most of us can tell of situations where we knew in advance that someone would say something or do something that we were thinking of at the moment. There are even those who say they can communicate with spirits on other planes of existence. (Sister Jan has been channeling for over twenty years with Romulus and others.)

Other people claim they can use their brain power to travel, absent their physical body. Many claim they have had an "out of body experience." Some of these reports come from near-death experiences, and others claim they can teleport themselves to other areas at will. The University of Michigan has done experiments with people for many years giving convincing reports of teleportation.

Some people can change physical things with only their thoughts. Uri Geller is able to bend spoons, in front of witnesses, using only the power of his mind. Another interesting thing is the Manhattan Project conducted by the military during the Second World War.

We must learn to accept that "we" are forever ourselves, not just the biology we call "our bodies." Dr. Bernie Siegel, a surgeon on the East Coast, wrote a book entitled *Love, Medicine and Miracles*. In this book Dr. Siegel reported on actual cases where people in their final days of an incurable illness were able to will themselves healthy just by believing they could. We definitely can have more control of our minds and lives than we have practiced. You and I can, and should, use our mind power to better advantage.

I started my career as a life insurance agent, making my living by cold-calling people from lists of new births, new homeowners, new marriages, and all the other things we used to qualify prospects with. (I quickly learned that getting referrals from my customers was an easier way to prospect.)

When people agreed to set up an appointment, I almost always saw them in their homes. I learned early on that I could tell in advance, even before getting into the house, if I was going to make a sale or not. If I could visualize myself writing the application as I was walking up to the door, I almost always succeeded. I don't know if that is any form of telepathy, but I do know that it worked, and my closing ratio was the highest in the office.

I have learned, over the years, that if I wanted something, I could get it, if I applied myself appropriately. Now what does that mean? When you have a goal, first it has to be a reasonable goal for you. Don't try to start with the near impossible and then say "I failed." Set short, intermediate, and long-term goals.

The next step is important. Write them down. By doing this you don't have the problem of trying to remember, or conveniently forgetting, what the goals were.

Then you must communicate the goals. Let others witness what you say you will do. Now you are less likely to back down when the going gets tough. Next, prepare yourself to achieve the goal. Go to school, study or practice.

Now the hard part begins. Believe in your heart that you have attained these goals. Foster that belief, and reinforce it until it is an integral part of your thinking. Belief, combined with education and experience, can bring you all the desired goals that you ever set for yourself. Of all these requisites, the most important is belief.

I have witnessed throughout the years the attainment of my most important goals, though they may not have happened just the way I planned. As I look back on my career, these accomplishments are not "just there." I brought them about with belief and will. I was able to obtain the number one position in sales of securities in a large national company. I was also able to build the number one agency in the United States for the same company, with more than 100 registered representatives.

It helps to set short-term goals as steps to accomplish your long-term goals. Set goals on a weekly or even daily basis, if you must. Know that a short-term failure will not deter you from reaching your long-term goals. Some people find that if they put their written goals away in a drawer and look at them later, they will achieve these goals. Others find that they must have their goals in front of them every day to review and confirm. Whichever way you choose to do it, remember, your mind is all-powerful and it can cause you to accomplish what you believe.

I have been married to Connie for thirty-two years and counting. She is the brave soul who agreed to share my life at a time when I still had three of my five children at home. She brought one daughter into our family. My children varied in age from ten to twenty-one, and Lisa was four. Can you imagine moving into a household with teenagers who had already formed their opinions on most things in the world? Most people tell me that I am a lucky man to have found someone willing to take on a ready-made family, and I agree.

Connie and I are having a most wonderful life, and I truly believe we have been in other incarnations as soulmates. She has taught me much about true love this time around. She always tells me, "You are a lucky man, Jim Counter," and I truly believe she is right.

But wait! Did I find Connie, or did she find me?

Connie had always wanted a big family. She married with the hope of fulfilling that desire, but it was not to be, as the marriage dissolved after only seven years. Connie and her daughter Lisa created a new household, and she became very comfortable with her status. She obtained a good job with the State of Minnesota that included the necessary benefits. She didn't need a "Man" to support her. She was happy with her life. Connie started attending a support group for divorced parents where she was encouraged to write down the qualities of a prospective partner. After completing the list, she put it in a drawer and promptly forgot about it.

Connie and I had been married for a couple of years when she came across the list again. As it turns out, I fulfilled all of the requirements.

The Universe will respond to your desires if you truly believe.

My experience has proven to me that what I think and believe will happen, really does happen, if I believe in my heart that it will.

Nelson Mandela said in his inaugural address: "Our deepest fear is not that we are inadequate, but that we are powerful beyond measure. It is our light, not our darkness, that most frightens us."

We are powerful! Beyond measure. We must learn to believe that we have that power.

Chapter 17

What Is God, and Who Are We?

Many people feel that we humans are created in God's image. Many also think that God looks like us in a physical way. We see Her/Him in a body with eyes, nose, ears, and all the other parts that our narcissistic minds can conjure. In the Christian Bible Jesus is said to be the son of God. Does this imply that God's son was created to look like his parent? Did Jesus not say that we were his brothers and sisters?

It is many people's belief that we are created in our physical form. I believe we are created in our spiritual form. Science has proven that all substance, all matter, is made up of vibrating energy.

It is my belief that God is the source of that energy. God is the spark that created the flame of creation. We indeed are a creation of the God Source. The energy of that God Source has provided all of creation.

I believe God created us in his image, which is spiritual. We are spirits of God. As God's spirits, we have the ability to use the unlimited energy of the God Source. I do not believe that God is a constant, but rather is constantly evolving. God is ever-changing by every experience, every action, every thought of Her/His creations, including us.

We humans, as spirits of God, have the power and the duty to create. We, as spirits, and as creations of God, are also constantly evolving. As a part of this evolutionary process our spirit must continue to acquire the knowledge of All That Is and all that can be.

Part of this learning experience can happen in what I have been calling the "Earth School." As spirits we can choose the use of this Earth School to help us learn and evolve. As spirits, we inhabit this physical form, this Homo sapiens entity called human. In order to make this a more productive learning experience, we do not bring with us all of our true spiritual knowledge, the knowledge of perfection.

In this Earth School we are given free will to do as we choose. Thus, we may, or may not, follow the planned potentials we set up for ourselves in any given incarnation.

Our spirit can reincarnate as many times as we feel there is opportunity to learn, or teach, in the evolutionary process. We plan our learning potentials between lives, while in spirit form. With our free will in this physical form we may follow the planned potentials, or not.

We all have an ever-increasing appetite for more. More of what? More of anything. More of everything. More good and more bad. All experience brings evolution.

Like some American Indians, I believe God is in everything and everything is made up of the God Source. We should respect all life forms. By the quantum definition, all matter is made up of this vibrating energy, just as we are. Does this mean everything is alive? Is the difference between us and that chair you are sitting on the fact that we have spirit and the chair does not? Some questions to ponder.

Chapter 18

Evolution, or Creation?

Does it have to be either/or? The science of evolution, as begun by Darwin, tells us that our physical form is constantly evolving and that all life has evolved from a seed amoeba. According to evolutionary theory, we humans have evolved over millions of years from this spark of life. Some religions teach that we were created, in our present form, by God. I believe both are true. There need not be an either/or. The question is, did God create us as spirits, or did He/She create us as Homo sapiens?

I believe that the God Source has created everything. The amoeba was from the God Source and God has never stopped creating. God has created the plants of the Earth, fishes of the ocean, the birds of the sky, and all the animals, including Homo sapiens. God has done this through evolution, as every substance is made up of the vibrating energy of the God Source.

I also believe that we are a creation of God, but in spirit form. God created spirits—us, as co-creators. Thus, in our true form, what we consider the human physicality is a blend of Homo sapiens—and us in spirit form. As spirits of God, we constantly observe God's creations. We, as co-creators, are constantly evolving as God is evolving. In our original spirit form, we observed this creation laboratory called Earth and saw many possibilities of learning.

As spirits of God, we are eager to learn and experience new things. We saw the possibility of learning while in physical form, especially if we could shield ourselves from God's knowledge with a temporary curtain. We had to know what it felt like to evolve without the knowledge of God.

We as spirit observed that the most advanced form of physical life on this Earth School was Homo sapiens. We made an agreement with this life form that we could enter it for all of the physical experiences through the senses of sight, taste, hearing, smell, and touch, but without the conscious knowledge of the God spirit.

As spirits of God's creation, we were indeed created in God's image. It is our incarnation in this physical form that makes us believe we have the limitations of the Homo sapiens body. Our physical existence is very temporary, while our spirit is eternal with the God Source. As spirit, we had to experience this existence through the senses of physicality.

The flower has beauty, but if not shared or seen, it is nothing, as it cannot see itself. When it is shared, it becomes the beauty that it is. We must also share our beauty to reach our maximum potential. Just as the flower has beauty in physical form, so we have beauty in spiritual form. Our spiritual evolution is enhanced by our physical experiences in this Earth School. It is the element of free will that makes each experience a quantum leap in our spiritual evolution.

Chapter 19

Heaven and Hell

At one time I believed that there was no heaven and no hell. I thought both were just creations of religion to keep people in line for the benefit of the church and society as a whole. We now see, through quantum theory and practice, that thoughts themselves are real. We create through our thoughts. We might say prayers themselves are our thoughts. We can create our future, indeed our NOW, by thoughts or prayers. If this be fact, then can we not create our own heaven and or our own hell just by believing in it?

Could it not then follow that groups, large or small, could also create their own heaven or hell? Can you think of examples of both in our current NOW? I can. Is it possible that we have both war (hell) and paradise existing at the same time? We can certainly point to examples of war in our NOW. We can also cite examples of paradise on Earth.

The choice is ours, individually, to be in either place. We are what we think. We can be in either heaven or hell in our NOW. It is our choice in this time frame, not some future time like the time we pass from this biology. But, you say, the people that are in a warring region of our world do not have a choice, as they cannot escape the place they are in. We must remember that all of us set up our potentials while between incarnations. We put ourselves in the place we are because it seemed like the best place for us to learn our desired lessons. Even if the physical world around us is hell, we need to remember that we can control how we react to it.

There are stories of people who have been prisoners of war who were tortured and put in conditions not fit for any living thing. Many of these people survived by thinking themselves into another place, their own paradise. Other people who were abused in other ways have also been able to endure by the same process.

Thus, I have changed my beliefs. I now believe that there is a heaven and a hell, and both exist now. It is our choice as to which we are in. We can be in paradise today. Just think about it. Being in paradise does not preclude our knowledge of war or hell. It just reinforces the fact that we made a choice to be where we are.

Chapter 20

Space Travel

When I think of space travel, my thoughts go to the limitations of my current biology. The mass that I have created, my body, has limitations on what I can do with it. My physical body is subject to maximum G-forces on acceleration and deceleration. For example, if I could accelerate the movement of my body to the speed of light, it would take much time, as the body can withstand only small multiples of G-force at any time. The same limitations would hold true on the slowdown, returning to where we are. Our thoughts of space travel, then, are limited by the physical limitations of our biology.

When I think about the true power of our mind and relate that to space travel, it becomes much easier to understand how space travel can work. I have been very fortunate in this incarnation to have been able to travel to many places on this wonderful Earth. I have mental pictures of each of these places and can go back to each and every one of them in just an instant, simply by thinking of it.

As I sit here writing this, I can also be in a hut in Tanzania, Africa, and then, in the next instant, on the Great Wall of China. The thought places me there with the same feelings as I had when actually in that place. No time elapsed in moving the thousands of miles from the hut in Tanzania to the Great Wall of China and then back to the chair where I sit.

While my physical body never moved, the real "I" moved thousands of miles, through thought. Thus, if I can move through thought (the real me, the spirit me), can I not then move (or travel) just as easily to other planets or galaxies or star systems?

In our true form (spiritual), we do not have the limitations of our biological mass or even of motion at the speed of light. We can "think" ourselves to any place at any time and back with no limitations and without the passage of time.

It may be a while before our fertile little human minds invent a machine that we can step into and be beamed from place to place as in *Star Trek*. The disassembly and reassembly of our molecular structure is beyond our current human limitations. However, as the true spirits of God that we are, we do not have these limitations. We created where we are and can also create any place we wish to be.

When my sister Jan completes her current project, perhaps we will have a better understanding of our biological limitations and how to overcome them. Until then, we will continue to test the limits of what we have created.

Chapter 21

How Are We Doing?

We all know that, as in magnetism, opposites attract and likes repel! Einstein said each action causes an equal and opposite reaction. Everything must be in balance. Electricity would not be possible without both positive and negative poles to move the power. Some would say that the whole universe is set up that way, even with positive and negative karma that is retained from one incarnation to the next.

If the above were accepted as truth, then is the Divine source also both positive and negative? Both good and bad, both love and hate? Well, you get the picture. Or is the Divine spirit total love? If total love, what is the definition of love? All good, or good and bad? Many questions, few answers, but something to think about.

Are we forever doomed to have the shadows so that we might know the light?

I think all of us can remember a negative experience, or many of them, that we have learned from. Is this experience really negative if we have grown from it? Would we be the same person with the same thoughts if we had only experienced positive transactions? I think not.

I believe that, to be balanced, we must see and experience both good and bad. I feel that in order to empathize with other people's experiences, we have to have a frame of reference. If we have been born with a silver spoon in our mouth, so to speak, can we really understand hunger?

I have had many wonderful experiences in this incarnation and some that did not seem all that great as I was going through them. I know you can relate. As time passes and we look back on all the experiences we have had, I think you will agree that each and every one has contributed to the person we are today.

When I first entered the life insurance business I was told that if I contacted forty people, I would receive thirty-nine *nos* for every *yes*. This seemed like a very negative way to make a living. What I learned was to look forward to each no, as it put me that much closer to a yes.

I guess what I am saying is that all of our experiences contribute to what we become. We incarnated to this Earth School to do just what we are doing, both good and bad. We set up our potentials before we got here, and with our free will we choose among these potentials to help us best evolve . . .

Keep your chin up. You are doing great.

Chapter 22

Is It Charity, or Is It Interference?

Currently we live in a society that considers charity a part of our daily lives. We seem to want to help the impoverished to have same the things we have, to be like US. I sometimes wonder if we are interfering with the life plan of other incarnates by trying to measure their lifestyle against ours. Should we always try to provide a house for the homeless? What about the aboriginal nomads? By providing houses for them, are we trying to change the very way they live or the customs they believe in? By trying to measure others' happiness or success by our standards, I believe we may be interfering with their life plan.

I grew up in a monetarily poor family. Most people today would say that there is much better furniture in a junkyard than what we possessed. Even after we had electricity installed in our home, we had no appliances such as a refrigerator, toaster, or electric clock. We had no running water or indoor toilets. There were no nickels and dimes to spend for treats or even get into the school basketball games. By today's standards we were way below the poverty level and eligible for charity from many potential sources. The point is, even without what people today would consider "necessities," I was happy. I did not realize that I was deprived of anything necessary. Many of our neighbors were not any better off than we were. We seemed to fit in with our peer group. Because there was no television to see how other people lived, I was content, and I really did not realize I was "poor." If charity stepped in to change my lifestyle, would I have had the same experiences by which I grew? Would I be the same person I am today?

I do not believe it is right to impose our standards on other people. I do believe we should always offer our love and understanding. We should always be willing to help out, to the extent we can, when asked. We should try to remember that we, each of us, wrote our own play in this incarnation, and we should allow others to live their own lives as they planned them. By imposing our good intentions on other incarnates, we may be smothering their ability to experience what their plan was for learning.

An offer to help is a good thing, but to impose requirements on the offer, not so good. Let people live their own lives as they planned them.

Chapter 23

The Trinity

Many religions have a version of the "Trinity" in their beliefs. While it may vary from one to another, the Christians call it the Father, the Son, and the Holy Ghost. All three seem to be equal in stature. In geometry, the equilateral triangle is the strongest structure, and it is used in girders and beams in the construction of large buildings and bridges. As we think about it, I am sure that we can come up with many groupings of three that are used to create strength.

In my belief, the Trinity is represented by the Source, the human biology, and the Higher Self. If I relate this back to the Christian version, the Father is the original source of energy that began creation. The Son is the human biology that holds a part of our spirit that was originally created by the Source. The Holy Ghost is our Higher Self, which is our home on the other side of the veil.

Each of the elements of the Trinity have the ability to create. Humanity to this point has had, by plan, a curtain dividing our current existence from our true knowledge of self. Thus, we do not remember who we really are and the true powers we possess. The new generation of humans are being born with more knowledge of who they are and their powers. Much is published today on the Indigos, the Crystals, the Stars, and the Phoenix generations of children. These children have been entering our Earth School since the 1980s. They are bringing with them more recall of who they are and the realization of the powers they possess.

I have twelve grandchildren and I see firsthand how they are much more advanced at an earlier age than I or even my six children were. I credit some of this advanced knowledge to their interest in the computers and handhelds that they now use, almost from birth.

Now be honest with me. How many of you can keep up with a seven-year-old on how to run today's household electronics? I seem to have trouble figuring out how to move around in, or find, programs on my television set. When my grandchildren come over, which fortunately is often, I have them give me lessons on how to run the various electronic gadgets that now seem to be everywhere in my home.

The world is moving much faster today, and the younger generations are more equipped to cope with this rapid change, largely because they are hardwired with this knowledge of who they are.

Don't worry! We have this knowledge too, but we may not be able to realize it until our next incarnation. See you on the next go-around.

Chapter 24

A Call to the Universe Times Two

Just before the end of the last millennium, Connie and I were contemplating getting a different place. We really loved our large Queen Anne home in New Richmond that I had purchased in 1976 before I moved from Milwaukee for my career change. Connie and our son, Scott, had conspired to "Connie-ize" the house with various additions and remodels, and both of us were pleased with the results. However, change seems to be a constant in this life, and we both had a desire to live "on the water." We began to look at lake cottages within a fifty-mile radius of our home.

After much thought and a lot of looking, we decided to put an in-ground swimming pool and hot tub in our yard. Considering our concern about the effort and expense of maintaining two separate properties, this seemed like a reasonable compromise. This did squelch the desire to be on the water, for a time, but alas, we kept looking for that one place we knew we needed, that place that would allow us to watch the sunset over the water. In the spring of 2000, we communicated our desires to a local real estate agent, so the search was on again. We had given the agent our parameters as to what we were looking for, including the price range.

We made a change in our thought process, so that instead of looking for a "lake cabin," we were looking for a "lake home." Yes, the desire we had for living on the water overcame the love we had for our Queen Anne. We looked at several places that fit our description, but saw nothing that really moved us. Then our real estate agent called us one day and said she had a place that we just had to see, and it had to be today, as there was a rumor of an offer being made on the property. It was slightly out of the price range we had quoted, but she really wanted us to look at it.

We went out that very evening to look at the lake home, and it was love at first sight. As we drove up the curving paved driveway to the house, I could not help but be moved by the two-and-a-quarter-acre lot with around a hundred mature pine trees on it. Some of them were over 100 years old. The home was on a lot high over Bass Lake with a wonderful vantage from its east bank allowing views of the setting sun over the water. With 175 feet of sand-gravel lakeshore and a gradual deepening of the water, it would allow for great swimming for the grandchildren.

And, oh yes! The house was nice enough that it did not need a great deal of Connie-izing. (Or so I thought at the time.) As we got out of the car we both knew this was our new home. We made an offer that same evening for $1000 over the asking price.

I tell this story in order to emphasize the power of sending a message to the Universe with the belief that it will come about. But wait, that's not all. Now we had to sell our home in New Richmond, and we had to sell it fast. We set a price to allow for the recovery of our investments, including the Connie-izing. We polished up everything and put it on the market immediately because we had already set a closing date on the Bass Lake property of thirty days out. The real estate market was strong, so we decided to sell our place directly rather than go through a real estate agent. We also knew that the Universe would send us a buyer.

We put a "for sale by owner" sign on our curb on a Saturday morning, and a couple from New Hampshire came to the door two hours later. He worked for 3M and was being transferred back to the home office in St. Paul. We had a full-price, no-contingent offer the very next morning, with the closing date to be one day before our closing on the Bass Lake home.

This is the Universe in action.

When we moved into our Bass Lake home, it was more like a fantasy world than real life. When I would drive home over the eight miles from my office, it felt to me as if I were driving to a vacation home. We would sit out on the deck with a cocktail listening to the breeze blow through the dancing pine trees. All of the wildlife in the area seemed to welcome us. The birds, squirrels, deer, a red fox with her kits, mating bull snakes, and the neighbor's cows lowing in the distance seemed to give us the feeling that we were a part of it all. The loons seemed to be talking to us each morning and evening with their lonely but comforting calls from the lake.

It was meant to be.

The lake home was a place to be shared and enjoyed by ourselves and our friends and family. We truly loved the socializing and used the home as a gathering place. Connie set up "Camp Connie" weekends for the grandchildren, and we began our collection of lake toys. I already had a fishing boat, but we added a pontoon, lifts, an extra dock, three trailers, and eventually a WaveRunner. (Connie became known as the fastest grandma on the lake.)

Scott and Connie got together on the planning process for a large wraparound deck with beautiful stone columns to maximize the views and the intimacy with nature. We had an electric lift installed on the lake bank especially for older folks (like me). But when the grandkids come over, I want you to guess who gets to use the lift and who walks the trail.

Scott even helped me plan an addition. With his help I got my thirty-by-forty "man shed" built to store all of our new toys. (All absolutely necessary, you know.) We now had our little piece of heaven to live in, love, and enjoy.

But now it's fifteen years later. The time just seems to fly when I am having fun. I retired four years ago at age seventy. Connie and I bought a motor home and we started traveling the country. In the last four years we have visited parts of forty-six states, trying to take in the attractions of each one. We have started to spend the winters in warmer climates, and I find that our interests now lie beyond our wonderful home on the lake. We seem to have developed the wanderlust. We are spending two months in Hawaii this fall, absent the motor home for obvious reasons, and plan to spend next summer in Alaska in our motor home.

We have become accustomed to living in much smaller quarters and do not miss the extra "stuff" that we seem to have acquired over the years. Our motor home clothes closet, note the singular, holds less than 10% of what we have in our house, and we find we do not need more. Now when we buy something, we have to discard something. What a novel idea!

We decided to sell our home on the lake. We are not sure of what area we will settle in next, but until we decide, we have our home on wheels. We expressed our plan to sell our lake home to several close friends and family, and soon received a call from a couple. We were not totally prepared to show it, wanting to stay in the house for one more year. But the couple said that this fit their purchase plans and they really wanted to come over to see the home as soon as possible. They came over, and like us, they found love at first sight. It was a nice evening, so after they had a chance to see the property we took them on a pontoon ride around the lake. We were explaining some of the history of the lake and talked about some of our wonderful friends that lived there. Before we got back to our dock they gave us a verbal full-price, no-contingent offer, with final closing to be just before we leave for Alaska next spring.

This is, indeed, the Universe in action. What we put out there does come back to us, just like the proverbial mirror.

As we sit on our deck under the dancing pines watching the sunset, we have lingering reservations about our decision to sell, but I know the new chapter of our life has some wonderful experiences for us to continue on our evolutionary paths.

Jims Afterward

When writing a book it is difficult to decide how to start and where to end. With my almost seventy-five years of life experiences it would be easy to continue the story for a few hundred more pages. It seems that each story, each experience, I relate back to brings up two more stories untold. I know that each of you reading this book could recall similar stories from your past that would make fascinating reading.

I hope you have enjoyed our version of reality. Aft er you have read through some of the topics in our book we hope that you will use it as a primer in your own learning journey. Each subject can be the root of a personal learning path or a group discussion. It is great to get together with groups of like mionded people as invariably Jan and I learn as much as we teach.

We were not raised with any specific religious beliefs, but the majority of the people in the area of the world where we live are of the Christian faith. With this, much of our reference to religion stems from that persuasion. There are many different religious sects and we have respect for all of them. We realize that there are many people who continue to need this guidance to stay on the right path.

We must keep in mind that the" right path" is different for each of us. We all write our own play and design the potentials that we experience in each incarnation. Jan nd I have learned to love every soul. We may not "like" some of them in this incarnation but we do love them for the pure spirits that they are.

We wish you "God speed" on your journey through forever.

Jims Acknowledgments

First and foremost I want to thank my wonderful wife Connie for picking me to share our life experiences. She has put up with me throughout the years as well as the time it took me to complete this book.

I want to thank my entire family for picking me to share this incarnation so that we might learn from and share our continued love for each other.

A special thanks goes to my daughter, Linda, for all the breakfast discussions on the many chapters over the last three years. You are a rock star.

Each of my six children, Scott, Diana, Jeffrey, Linda, Amy and Lisa have provided living material, support and experiences for these pages, and for a happy life.

I thank my publisher Deb Jacobson of Prarie Pond Publishing for all the help and guidance in the process of bringing this book to print.

Finally, I want to thank co-author and sister Jan Cassidy for directing and prodding me throughout my life too stay on track in the learning process in this, and probably other incarnations.

Jan's Story

Chapter 1

The Beginning

I was born in Wabasha, Minnesota, in 1936. My brother Bobby was born in July 1937 and died of pneumonia in January 1938. I vaguely recall his being there and then being gone. Mom changed after Bobby's death and became stricter and more unbending with me. Looking back, I can understand what she must have been going through. Later in life I wondered why she didn't draw me closer, value more the child she had left. It seems that she must have, in some way, blamed me for his death. In our family her mother, my grandmother, valued the boys more than the girls, and that could be the answer. I seem to remember that after Bobby's death, Mom was gone for a while. My guess now would be for therapy, although it has never been mentioned in the family.

I have good and bad memories of life with both my parents. The winter I was three, Mom took the sled in one hand and me in the other and we set out for the hill behind our house. I was so scared. As I looked down that hill it seemed to descend forever, but Mom was holding on to me, so that is a good memory. Then, from the age of two, there were the spankings I endured when she lost her temper. Some of them were pretty bad, more like beatings. My mother's mood could change in a moment and go in an opposite direction, and there never seemed to be a clear signal for when it would happen. After I grew older I began to retreat into myself. I decided that trying my best to disappear was the safest way to get along.

Sometimes in the summer, up until I was five, Daddy would put me on his shoulders after supper and walk down the hill to the little neighborhood grocery store, where he would buy me an ice cream cone. I don't have any memories of Daddy spanking me or even scolding me for anything in those first five years. He called me his little angel girl. I have vague memories of sitting with Daddy on the back porch while he cracked black walnuts for me to eat, and of eating limburger cheese with him out there because Mom wouldn't allow it in the house.

Then in April 1941 my brother Jim entered my life, and it was love at first sight. I was four and a half, and I instantly became his voluntary watch dog. When he cried, I talked to him. When he crawled, I crawled by his side. Later I became his playmate/sparring partner. We fought over anything and everything between ourselves, but had each other's backs when anyone else threatened either of us. Jim's birth was the first major event in my life, and the second happened later that same year, when we moved away from Wabasha, the only home I had ever known. This move foreshadowed a total change in our family and in my life.

Pearl Harbor shocked the nation into war, and my parents decided to move to Duluth, Minnesota, to seek war jobs. The country was just coming out of a depression, and people would pack up everything and move hundreds of miles to get in on "the big money."

The Wabasha years proved to be the only time in my life when I felt reasonably safe and nurtured. From then on, as each year went by, I withdrew further as my only protection from a world I couldn't understand. I learned that if I stayed in the shadows, I could sometimes go unnoticed. I believe that this lonely shadow world was what first began to foster my interest in things that didn't quite make it to my conscious awareness— things more sensed than seen or heard.

Both my parents soon got jobs in Duluth. This signaled the end of a life that I was never to see again. Daddy began to change into someone I didn't know and learned to fear. Mom got pregnant again with my brother David, and Daddy, not wanting the baby, let his feelings be known, loudly and often. When David was two years old, he fell out of the car and developed epilepsy. The seizures grew so bad that when he was four, Mom had to put him into a state hospital. He never returned home, and died there many years later.

Mom worked days and Daddy worked nights, so that meant we had many sitters. Most of them were good to us, but several could be classified as downright cruel. However, we had no recourse when a sitter treated us badly, because neither parent wanted to hear about it. As time went on my parents drew further and further apart, and Daddy began to drink more heavily, which changed him into someone I barely knew. Mom began to go out with friends she met at work and I think Daddy's jealous rages were not always so far off the mark. I suffered abuse: mental, emotional, physical, and sexual. It was then that I came to the conclusion that I couldn't trust any adult. That distrust grew until it totally colored my outlook and ruled my life. I seldom had a close friend, probably because I was afraid to share that much of myself. As I became more withdrawn, my ability to form friendships with other children became nonexistent. The memories of my school years seemed like a loop painfully repeating the fact that I was nobody and would never be accepted by the somebodies. Each succeeding year became a carbon copy of the last, repeating the bullying and abuse that only grew worse as time passed. I began to live more and more inside myself. Then my parents divorced and my life changed again.

Chapter 2

Life Brings a Major Transformation

When Mom eventually left Daddy, she moved us to Fargo, North Dakota, where her parents lived. Their small apartment was hardly sufficient for them let alone us. Mom wasn't well educated, but she finally got a job as a waitress. Grandma wanted us out, so we badly needed a place to live. Mom's job didn't pay much, so the only house she could afford to rent was located in the red light district. The house had no bathroom so we used a pee pot and emptied it in a bathroom across the alley in the old men's hotel. We ate a lot of cold hot dogs, but it wasn't a bad life, even without financial support from Daddy. It was the best that Mom could provide.

It seemed to me that she was never home, and looking back now, I think she must have worked double shifts much of the time. Jim and I were eleven and seven, and having so much unsupervised freedom gave us plenty of opportunities to go places and do things that were not really acceptable for kids our age. We would go down to the Red River and throw rocks at the giant sewer rats that came out of the mouth of a huge pipe that drained into the river. It was fun at the time, but now I cringe to remember their squealing and their big yellow teeth.

We had other equally interesting amusements, and for the first time in my life I had a friend. In fact, I had two friends; twins who were from Mexico. Their mom made the best tortillas I've ever had. They had a cookstove that burned wood and when it was hot enough she dipped her hand in the batter and spread it over the scorching metal. I recall that the palm of her hand had huge thick calluses from the hot stove top. In moments the crisp tortilla was ready to eat and I got to eat many of them. I learned a lot about being a friend from them, but also gained head lice, which didn't make Mom happy. She treated my head with kerosene and a fine-tooth comb. She got rid of the lice, but the burning of the kerosene and the painful scalp scraping are not among my most pleasant memories.

As we were the only kids living in that neighborhood and the ladies of the night watched over us when Mom was working. One Saturday evening when Mom was working extra hours, a loud knocking came at the door, and when I answered it a man stood there trying to hold his balance against the door frame. I was scared because I could tell he was drunk. Just then fat Lizzy, who plied her trade in the house next door, came out to see what the noise was. In an instant she had assessed the situation, grabbed a broom, and jumped off her porch, and with skirts flying, chased the man off our porch. She followed him as he staggered down the alley trying desperately to get away, and Lizzy, overweight as she was, kept up with him while bashing him with the broom. I can still hear her screaming, "Ya get yaself outa heah now, and if ah evah ketches ya sniffin' 'roun' them little 'uns agin, I'll kill yo' ass." I think back now on how lucky we were to have those ladies' caring protection.

Something occurred that summer that made me begin to wonder whether things might exist beyond my conscious awareness. Could there be an unseen world all around me that could be sensed but not seen or touched? It happened during the only time in my life that I ever got to go to camp. Each summer the Salvation Army sponsored the neighborhood children for a week at a local Lake. Mom somehow came up with a dollar for me to spend at the camp canteen, and as the bus left Fargo, I was so excited. When we arrived at the camp there were huge trees surrounding the cabins, and the lake was very blue and beautiful. Everything about it was so far beyond my experience that the whole week was more like a dream than reality. One of the things that impressed me was that my bunk mate had a pet garter snake and took it everywhere with her. She even slept with it.

There I had my first brush with a world that captured my interest, then and forever after. A world that has been sometimes frightening, but always calling me back to learn more. During one evening church service the final prayer left me feeling as if I had been touched by something I couldn't explain. Later I slipped back into the empty chapel to sit and wonder about this strange feeling. Suddenly the quiet intensified and my hair stood on end. I was paralyzed, rooted to the seat, with the distinct sense that I was not alone. I seemed to hear soft music and faint whispered words that I couldn't quite understand. I felt fear but also awe and wonder. I remember thinking that this was a church and that whatever was happening to me could not harm me. After a while it stopped and I went back to the cabin, trying to understand what had happened.

At that time I was just beginning to be exposed to organized religion and the many new concepts it brought into my world. I read the Bible and went to Sunday school and church when I could, but more often there was no one to take me, and we usually lived too far away for me to walk. I read a chapter of the Bible to Jim every night. I didn't skip any words because I was afraid that if I did, they would have been just the ones that would explain things to me. We were both heartily sick of the "begats," and were just sure that we would never get to the end of them. But we did. Sadly though, I never did get any of those definitive answers I so eagerly desired. In the following years many things occurred, good changes and some not so much, but I never lost an inner certainty that the truth that I was seeking awaited me, somewhere.

That belief fostered a continuing curiosity about the unseen that was to grow through the years, and at nineteen, trying to make sense of it all, I began to ask serious questions. My first was about Genesis, where it said that in the beginning Adam and Eve were the first people to be formed by God and that they had three sons, Cain and Abel in quick succession. After a while Cain got the idea that God had a greater love for Abel, so he murdered him, initiating the first recorded homicide. God did not destroy Cain for that, but banished him from Eden. The Bible then states that Cain went to the Land of Nod and took a wife. Now, if Eden was the first place God created as a home for humanity and they were the first humans, then where was the Land of Nod, and how did Cain find a wife there? I asked my questions of quite a few different ministers and pastors and got answers such as, "Some things we must take on faith," and, "Well, they were the first humans with souls." With these explanations, each more ambiguous than the last, it seemed that they would always skirt my questions, so I decided that I would look for answers by following my own path. I figured that something was seriously wrong with this picture if these people were attempting to teach something they seemed to know so little about. So after years of searching and asking questions that seemed to have no answers, I decided that the Old Testament of the Bible is a marvelous history book. The New Testament with the words of Jesus is, I believe, an everlasting teaching example to humanity promising what we humans are capable of attaining. Each of us is a spiritual work in progress, and growing at our own speed.

Chapter 3

Another Move Brings a Difference and Yet More of the Same

In 1948, when I was twelve, we moved from Fargo to Palisade, Minnesota, to a property that had been homesteaded by our great-grandparents on the bank of the Mississippi River. It was kept in the family to shelter members who were in trouble until they could get back on their feet. There we had the river and an old barn to play in, but it was definitely a trade-off. We moved in during the spring flood when the river was very high. It covered the pipe that brought wonderful crystal-clear icy water from the artesian well deep underground, so for a while our only access to drinking water was the river. We had to dip water from a side pool with a bucket, carry it to the kitchen washstand, and try to sweep the mosquito larvae aside with the dipper to get a drink. We had no heat except that which came from the wood-burning kitchen stove, and one kerosene lamp sufficed for light—that is, when we had kerosene. Mom had no car and very little money, so when a farmer offered to donate milk to us, Jim and I walked half a mile up the road once a week to his farm, and, although it was difficult, we each carried back home a filled gallon jar.

One night a man came to visit Mom, and she began telling him some stories about the supernatural things that were supposed to have happened in the area, and in our house in particular. I was sitting back in a corner listening, becoming more afraid by the minute. Finally Mom noticed me and told me to go to bed. As we had only the one lamp, I would have to stumble my way up in the dark to the room that Jim and I shared. By that time I was petrified with fear, and when I said that I was afraid, Mom kind of exploded. I believe she was posturing to impress the man, but perhaps she really didn't realize how it would affect me. She said that I needed to get over my fear of the dark right then and there and forced me to go outside without a light and walk all the way around the house, rapping on each window as I passed it to prove I had done what she ordered.

One of the ghost stories that she had just told was of the poker games that were said to have gone on in the basement of the house many years before. The story was that the last game between some men who worked felling trees for my great grandfather ended in an argument over the cards, and four men were killed that night. Forever after it was said that their ghosts haunted the cellar, playing games of poker that always ended in murder. I had to go past the ground-level entrance to the basement to reach the rear windows. The cellar by then was no more than a room partially filled with dirt, with the door lying flat on the ground, rotten and in pieces. Not being able to see my way, I tripped over it and fell partway down the cement steps, getting pretty well skinned up. I just knew that any minute I would be grabbed and dragged down into that pitch-black hole and killed. My heart was pounding and I had never been so scared, but I managed to crawl back up and finally got around the house and limped back inside. Mom just said, "Now, go to bed." I didn't dare tell her I was hurt.

That man became our stepfather. I guess there's not a lot I can say about him. I avoided him as much as was humanly possible. Mom cared for him, and we did not. However, he had four small children that Jim and I came to love. His mentality was not very high, and he could be a real bully. He was easily led and couldn't seem to figure out the proper way of interacting with others. He and Mom were good together though, because she liked to be in charge and he needed to be led.

Chapter 4

I Marry Once, Twice, Three Times

The years passed, some fairly good, and others not so much. What little communication Mom and I ever had stopped when I was ten. Something happened that I couldn't forgive her for, and there was never a good understanding between us. When I was fifteen Mom realized that she had lost her total control over me when we argued about me staying in town for a ball game. She took off her leather belt, smacked me with it a few of times and got absolutely no reaction. I didn't cry, I didn't try to get away I just stood and looked at her. I later learned that after that she was planning to send me to a girls' school where I would have remained until I was eighteen.

This was the same scenario that she had followed when she had had a baby at thirteen. Back in 1930 it was a terrible stigma to have an illegitimate baby, so the family, to avoid shame, sent her to live with an aunt in another state. Well, the baby was taken away at birth, and my mother was sent back home. She wasn't welcome there and so was sent to a school that took in wayward girls, where she stayed until she was eighteen. She then married the first man who asked her, my father. She was eighteen and Dad was thirty-eight.

The summer I was fifteen her sister, my aunt, came to visit from another state and learned of Mom's plan to get rid of me. The aunt said no, that wasn't going to happen, and she took me back to her home. I stayed there until I was sixteen, at which time I returned to Minnesota. Mom introduced me to a man who worked with my stepfather, and with her written permission, I married him and we immediately moved to Iowa. He turned out to be an alcoholic batterer, and the marriage didn't last long, but it did produce one wonderful child.

During the first years, though, I experienced some things that I could not explain. We lived in a house where several unexplained incidents occurred that fed my growing awareness of, and interest in, the unknown. Two of these were witnessed by others and two by only me.

Jim was fourteen in 1955 and came to spend the summer with me in this house. One night, after we had shut the television off and were talking before bed, the picture of a man from mid-chest up formed on the screen. We tried everything we could to make it go away. We unplugged the set and disconnected the antenna, but the figure stayed on the screen all night. By morning it was gone, but Jim was pretty frightened because he was sleeping on the couch in the same room. He said he had pulled the blanket over his head and prayed. That was a one-time occurrence, but four people witnessed it. The next day I called every TV repairman in town, and the nearest anyone came to an explanation was that it was an image frozen on the screen from the last program we watched. Now that couldn't be, because we hadn't watched anything that even remotely resembled that image. No one has ever been able to explain it to the satisfaction of those of us who witnessed it.

The second incident in that house, like the first, happened only once. It was when I was home alone with my baby daughter, my husband having gone out to his favorite tavern. We lived in the downstairs apartment and I was rocking my daughter to sleep when I heard footsteps overhead. The upstairs apartment was empty at the time, and I had a clear view of the front door and hallway that both apartments used, so I knew no one had gone up there. If there is such a thing as having your heart in your throat with fear, that's where mine was. After a while, though, I finally found the courage to sneak up the stairwell. Just as I got to the top, the footsteps stopped. I did a very, very quick look around, found nothing, and went back downstairs. I no sooner got settled in the rocking chair with my daughter when the steps began again. This time I reacted a little faster. Again the footsteps stopped as I got up there. This time, summoning my courage, I walked through the rooms, and again, no one was there. After that there was only silence the rest of the night. The footsteps never returned, much to my relief.

Another time, just before my husband came home from work, a water glass that had been missing for several months suddenly reappeared on the table, which had not been set for the meal yet. I had not heard nor seen anything as I worked at the stove, but when I turned to look at the table, there it was. I was pretty frightened, but finally picked it up, and there was not a fingerprint or anything else on it. It was very real and it had certainly not been there a moment before.

The final occurrence was a medicinal odor that would sometimes drift through the house. It seemed to be strongest in the room we used as a bedroom, but I could smell it in every room. I called the landlord and told him about it because I was afraid it might be something dangerous. He told me that I was imagining it, and I told him I certainly was not. He said that the next time it happened I was to call him and he would come. When he did grin left his face. I said, "Now do you smell something, or not?" He said yes, and added that the house had always smelled like that before his wife passed away. He said she had been bedridden for two years and she had died right there in the room we used for a bedroom.

I never again experienced anything like the happenings in that house. My marriage continued to crumble because of the drinking and the beatings. I filed for divorce in 1960 and moved my daughter and myself to a small apartment. During the divorce my mother took my daughter back to Minnesota until I could get on my feet. Not being in the best shape emotionally and having nowhere to turn for support, within a few months I married again. I probably wouldn't have done that, but in 1960 the agencies for helping single mothers were not nearly as common nor as helpful as they are today, and I felt I had nowhere to turn. As I look back, I can see that what was driving me then was the fear of trying to make it alone and failing and losing my daughter. The other strong incentive was the knowledge that if I married again, I could bring my daughter back home.

After four years I had two more children, and my husband had moved us back and forth across Iowa twelve times in four years. I again filed for divorce. That one too was nasty. Now I had three children to take care of, with a low-paying factory job and no other support. I was again haunted by the fear that I wouldn't be able to take care of them and would lose them. In the sixties there were very few alternatives open to me. Nowadays a single mother in that position has the city, state, and federal governments to turn to for help. I struggled, sliding backward, always hoping for a miracle.

Within a few months I met my third husband and fell in love. He turned out to have one love in his life, and that was alcohol, but still this marriage was to last for many years. I finally couldn't stand the drinking binges and the other women associated with them. The hurt they caused was growing, and yet I couldn't leave him. I kept thinking that maybe someday he would stop drinking, and what a wonderful life we would have then. I began pulling into myself again, and as I did I began losing the will to try anymore. I wanted nothing more than to die and go home and leave this life behind. I tried many things to bring myself out of that slump. Looking to find comfort and advice, I even tried to establish a tie with the other side through automatic writing. I had read about mediums doing that. I did seem to make contact, but it didn't amount to much. I was never sure whether it was real or just my wishful imagining.

By this time the kids were grown and gone and I had no hope left. My husband was only working half the time because he wouldn't stay sober long enough. I knew about things that went on when he was drunk but because I couldn't leave him I was going to choose death. I was sitting at the typewriter one day and trying to compose suicide note when suddenly my fingers began to move completely on their own, The movement was very hesitant at first and I just stared at the typewriter, not really understanding what was happening as my fingers felt their way among the keys. Then I read what was being typed so painstakingly, "I am Romulus." Was as I creating something from my own mind? Was I crazy? Was it my subconscious trying to assure me that life could hold something for me besides suicide? My fingers began to slowly move again, and to say that I was stunned is a real understatement. Romulus assured me that we could communicate if I would sit at the typewriter each day. That was all I got the first time, but it was plenty to set me thinking about something besides suicide.

The rest of that day my mind was filled with all the fears that I had gathered during my life. They crowded in, and although I tried to face them one by one, I was under siege from every front. Oh God, was this the Devil making contact and, if so, will I go to hell for talking to him? Was this an evil spirit who would take over my mind as I had seen in movies and books I had read, and even if it wasn't, did I have the courage to pursue this blind contact? Had I finally gone round the bend and would I wind up my life in an asylum? How would I tell others about this contact? (As it turned out, I did not mention it to another soul until several years later, and then the first person I haltingly shared it with was my brother Jim.)

Now, Jim and I have always had a special bond that began when we were children, and even though we were separated fairly early in life, that bond has grown throughout our lives. He has proved to be a steadying influence on me in many situations, and I have tried to bring any new knowledge I found to his attention so we could learn together. He was the one person whom I felt would understand and accept this new area of life that I was entering. This proved to be true, and through the years we have shared our knowledge and insights. Romulus said that the reason we decided to incarnate together this in this life was that we would give strength to each other as we followed the special interests we had in common.

After Romulus and I began communicating, life changed for both Jim and me. One thing this contact did was to cement our growing belief that there was more to being human than we had ever suspected. From then on we both looked for any knowledge that would enlarge our growing beliefs. We shared the insights that we gained, and my communication with Romulus changed our lives in major ways and forever.

My personal feelings also changed in so many ways. As my trust in Romulus grew, I found that for the first time in my life I could accept myself as I was. As I learned to trust myself, I felt a growing trust in my life's journey, and so I began trying to live rather than just exist. After I started to depend on myself, my marriage lasted another twenty-five years, not always happily, mind you, but still I learned many truths that I needed for my developing insight.

Well, back to my first contact with Romulus. After a long, sleepless night, I decided to try again. Like Alice in Wonderland, in spite of the strangeness of the situation and my fear of the unknown, I would go onward to see what lay ahead. After all, I really didn't have much else left in my life. I sat at my typewriter the next day wondering whether it would happen again. It did, and it lasted longer than the day before. I was told that if I would keep communicating every day, in time the link would get stronger. So I did, and it did.

Chapter 5

I Begin to Accept Romulus as Real

As time went on I felt that I was being helped on a level of which I was not consciously aware. This went on for months, and many times the thoughts and teachings coming out of my typewriter almost seemed to be things that I was remembering rather than ideas I was hearing for the first time. I have noticed through the years that when there is a new truth for me to explore, I am led to the idea in some way. Many times I have been passing a bookstore with no conscious thought of wanting a book but have entered anyway and gone straight to a particular section and saw a book that almost said, "Buy me." I always find that this will be the first step down a particular road that Romulus wants me to travel. Other times I get hints or even direct references. Or I'll hear a word or have a thought over and over. I'll see something wherever I look that I have never given conscious consideration to before. In these ways I am led to certain prompts that point me toward more new thoughts, thoughts that finally lead to a new grasp of reality that I did not formerly possess.

Now I'd like to add an explanation here about Romulus. I was never once forced or coerced into communicating with him, and in all our years together he has never tried to influence me in any way to do anything of which I didn't approve. I have never been afraid of him. I have always been totally free to respond, or not, and everything that he has taught me has been for my benefit. I will realize a truth I hadn't known before or a changed belief or a way of looking at a thing, and he will say, "*Very good. You have learned well.*"

I, of course, have no conscious knowledge of many of these lessons, and when I one day compained he said, "It is *your higher self with whom I deal. This alloiws you to absorb the results of the lessons as innate truths. You walk a path that began when all were new to your world. All are, through lifetime after lifetime, trial after trial, on the path toward awakening and total awareness in this reality. This awakening of total awareness will bring the next step in human evolution.*"

If I were to sum up the way Romulus teaches, it would be to quote from Khalil Gibran, the great Lebanese poet.

If the teacher is indeed wise, he does not bid you enter the house of his wisdom, but rather leads you to the threshold of your own.

Chapter 6

Romulus Takes Things to a New Level

One day, several years after the first contact, Romulus asked me a question that seemed simple enough, until I tried to answer it. It was, "*What do you want most in the world?*" Now I had daydreamed of many things during my lifetime and actively pursued none of them. I had thought that the one thing that I most wanted to bring into my life was being a writer. I always felt that I had stories to tell, and I tried, but I never seemed to finish anything. I thought about his question for a long time. Finally I realized that my life had been about searching for truth, so that's what I told him. The thing that I wanted most in this world was to find the truth of existence.

He merely said, "*Very good,*" but I got the distinct feeling that he was pleased with my answer. He said that I must not allow fear to direct my actions. He further stated that fear is a self-imposed wall or limit that has no place in reality except the place we give to it. That wall is built on fear caused by negative reactions to life experiences, and he would help me to overcome these perceptions that had intimidated me most of my life.

This proved to be true, and so I gradually began to value life as a gift rather than a burden. To accomplish this I began an intense period of trying to raise my vibrational level to facilitate our communications. I was told that the way it works is that the teachers and guides must lower their vibrations, and we need to raise ours in order for active communication to take place. One of the first things I was taught was to pull up all the negative emotions associated with the worst experiences in my life and relive them, over and over, until I had drained all emotion from them, until it seemed as if they had happened to someone else. It took a long time and was one of the hardest things I have ever done. Toward the end, things that had happened to me that I had forgotten, things I had totally pushed out of my conscious mind, began to emerge. That time of my life was very painful, but in the end, the catharsis it brought was not only healing but changed my whole worldview. I began to feel a confidence that was wonderfully welcome. It was the beginning of a sense of self-worth that had never been nurtured in any of my life's experiences until then. It seems that in order to reach this plateau of self-worth, all the negatives, or as Romulus called them, burdens, accrued throughout this life and indeed many lifetimes must be, in his words, "ordered to understanding," and this is what I did, with his help. It seems that each part of my whole self that had been shattered into fragments by negative events in this life, plus my reincarnational selves, must again come together to form a complete entity.

He said that when I am aware of the total proof, that proof being the awareness of all the parts of me, I will be ready to go on. He explained that this shift in world consciousness is something that has been preordained. It seems that there are many on that side who are gathering to help all who are ready to accept this enlightenment, which is the next step in human evolution. It has been a long journey to join my splintered minds, and Romulus is always there when I question or am in need of assurance, and I have the amazing awareness that I am never alone.

Romulus said early on that he was my teacher and was here to help me raise my vibrational level in this lifetime. Much later he asked me if I would be willing to conduct an experiment with him. I asked, "What sort of experiment?" He said that we would try to raise my vibrational level as high as we could and see what would happen. I, of course, said, "What do you mean, see what will happen? Has this never been done before?" He told me that it had not in exactly this way, but that it was supposed to happen and would enhance the next step in human evolution. He said that some throughout history had been born with higher vibrations, but to begin from so little and try to purposefully increase them was an experiment, and that we would try. Many others all over the world who are establishing contact with the other side are part of the new advance in humanity's long and laborious climb toward the freedom that is being earned as we help to raise the vibrations of all mankind. Raising human vibrations would in effect allow humans to consciously control the energy that makes up everything in our world, including our bodies. In other words, to consciously create. I took this shocker away from the typewriter and thought it over for days before returning with my answer. Having read some other channelings, it seemed that many of them hinted at much the same thing, so I gave my permission and my lessons began.

Chapter 7

Who or What Is God?

The vast God energy is everything: all that exists. There is nothing except the God energy. Picture an unimaginably large container compartmentalized into uncountable small cells, as in a honeycomb, with each representing a world. The whole is composed of pure energy, and the cells vibrate at different levels. Each of these worlds is slightly different, and between each of them is a veil that normally prevents them from being aware of anything beyond their immediate reality. Their self-imposed limits effectively separate them from knowing anything outside their own range of vibrations. Our chosen experiences before we are born decide which world we will inhabit in any given life. One of the first questions I asked was, "Who or what is God, and who or what are we?" Here is the answer I received.

"God is the fundamental energy from which springs all being, massless but creating mass, without beginning or end, the source of all existence. You constantly seek after, turn to, "The Source", and yet "You" are the source. You do not, as yet, realize your own power and as, "The Source", you constantly search for your awakening, the key to your power, which will bring enlightenment that leads you into the next stage of your evolution.

You do not realize that the key is in your hands right now. You need only search out the door. You are meant to grow and evolve into the foreverness that lies ahead of you. You have a destiny that you are growing into. You advance with every truth that you successfully stamp with your own knowing. Each time you bring a personal truth, it is referred to as a "pattern", and it becomes knowledge that everyone can tap into. To put your own stamp on a truth is to create, face, and solve a situation in your own totally unique fashion. You each have lived many lifetimes in physical reality. That seems a very long time to you, and yet it is such a small part of your destiny Because you have no beginning and no ending. Your lives in this reality are measured by your evolvement toward truth. You constantly seek after, turn to "The Source", but you do not yet realize that you are "The "Source.

The years and the lessons went on, and as I would come to some new knowledge, or change my worldview a bit, Romulus would express approval and begin the next lesson. It has been many years and many lessons and we are still working at it, but now the assurance is that we are reaching some sort of step that will allow me to see beyond the veil and become aware of two worlds at one time.

This explanation I will now share came to me once when I was in meditation. I don't expect everyone to agree with me, and I have nothing to base this on except an inner feeling that it could be the beginning. Not of the primal energy which has always existed, but of the aware God that we look to as our Creator.

IT stirred.

The roiling energy became stronger as ALL THAT IS began to feel unsatisfied.

IT longed for—what?

The awareness was growing stronger.

Sensing changes, the realization came that IT must do something, become more, but more than what?

IT was becoming aware of BEING.

With that first awareness came a feeling, tenuous at first, a feeling that IT must create.

As these faint sensations began to solidify into direction, IT sensed a beginning of something, something that had never before existed. IT was creating a SELF.

And so the Primal Energy, the ALL THAT IS, came to self-awareness. That energy became GOD.

And GOD began to give birth to worlds.

Then, into these worlds, GOD seeded spirits as parts of the wholeness.

And these spirits would create in their own right, ensuring their state of always becoming and thus the forever becoming of GOD.

And GOD created both those who were born to the worlds and those never to know this birth, who would watch and give aid to those on their journey to discover who and what they are.

And GOD learned from these creations. And the GOD energy grew as creation grew. And the growing brought meaning.

And the meaning created emotions, the foremost of which was a total and unconditional love for all ITS creations.

Through this love was born the discovery that GOD was love.

And from that first knowledge of love was opened to mankind the door of forever.

Forever creating and facing the countless scenes to which each spirit could choose to respond in its own unique way.

There can be no question of growing or traveling back to rejoin GOD. We are already a part of GOD. We need not work for a place we already own. Our birthright is assured.

Somewhere, within each of us, lies the comfortable knowledge that we are never alone. We are forever safe because we are always in direct contact with our creator. I am not saying that this is truth, I merely say that the insight came to me in meditation. As I believe that we are all contained within GOD, it filled a need in me to bring truth to myself. To me, GOD is everywhere and nowhere. GOD is the quantum soup that makes up all of consciousness.

We are a part of that consciousness; thus, in a way, we are GOD. We cannot separate what makes up the unique ME from the consciousness of ALL THAT IS. We cannot separate ourselves from a spouse, a child, family, neighbors, the animals, the plants—the very Earth itself. Everything in existence is in, and of, ALL THAT IS, our CREATOR, our GOD.

Mankind is now in a period of evolution that calls for a tremendous leap forward, and we are in the process of doing just that. When Jesus taught love and forgiveness, he introduced a jump in human evolution that was to raise the collective vibrations of all humanity. Now is the time that another such jump in evolution is in the process of again bringing a new vibratory rate to all of humanity and the very Earth itself. This is happening all over the world and at an ever-increasing rate. Through contact with teachers and guides, we are moving into the next phase in our forever lives.

Ultimately, we are to become consciously aware of the veils between ourselves and the other realities. We are to see through and overcome the self-imposed limits and go on to discover our next adventure on the path of forever becoming for ourselves and for our Creator.

Anatole France, the great French novelist, once wrote something that, in my mind, describes the emotional effects of the changes humanity is now going through. He said, *"All changes, even the most longed for, have their melancholy. For what we leave behind us is a part of ourselves. We must die to one life before we can enter another."*

Each day as we become more and more aware of the truth, we change our outlook, our worldview, our actions and reactions toward ourselves, our brothers and sisters, and the Earth.

Some are moving at a greater speed than others, but sooner or later we will all move on to the next adventure, ensuring a continuous becoming for ourselves and for our Creator.

Chapter 8

Time

Is time really speeding up, as it seems to be doing for many of us? One day it came to me that time seems to pass much faster now than it did years ago. Some people would say that is just because with age you take on many responsibilities and interests that you don't deal with when summer vacation from school seems like a year, while at fifty a day sometimes begins and ends within several hours, and a year can seem like a couple of months. I was puzzled, because I felt that there must be a better explanation than that, so I asked Romulus how there could be anything including life without time. He then went into the subject of time and why we need it.

> *"Time does not exist. It flows neither backward nor forward. It is you who, in creatively imagining your lives, bring into being the illusion of the passage of time in order to accomplish the tasks that you have entered physical reality to experience. I have told you that time is the part of your reality that allows you to create situations, interactions, decisions and choices. This means that you deliberately create aging and illness, death and disease, love and self-sacrifice in order to experience the effects of your decisions. Your entire lives in this reality are based upon the passage of time. Your responses contribute to a constant state of becoming more than you were. As you learn to react to your creations with love, your vibrations become more harmonious, and this raises them to a higher level. As you gain these higher levels, time does*

indeed pass faster for you. The reason that you and so many others like you are accepting communications from this side now is that all life and indeed the very earth itself are in the process of raising their vibrations. This will cause a change that creates a very different way of life for all. It has definitely begun. Along the way there will be many hardships, but when the old finally gives way it will bring a great new concept on which to base lives on earth. It has definitely begun.

This seemed like a better explanation, and it just felt right. To me it pointed out the promise that there is an important reason for the things that are now happening in the world and to me personally. One of the ideas that we must try to get our minds around is that time, as we know it, does not exist everywhere. And yet it seems that everything we know, the entire world in which we live, depends on our use of time. We use time for our appointments. We gauge our age, a prison sentence, the years spent in school, by the measuring stick of time. But it is baffling, the idea that TIME DOES NOT EXIST. It has no meaning in the great NOW outside our narrow physical limits. There everything is happening at once. Pretty hard to imagine, but imagine it we must if we are to continue our spiritual journey.

Chapter 9

Just How Real Are We?

Quantum theory says that we and all our surroundings are holograms, and outside the physical world the past, present, and future all exist as one. Now that's really tough to stretch your mind around, because to ourselves we are real. When we touch our bodies, or a tree, or another person, we touch something solid and alive.

These things that our spirits have created from basic energy comprise our physical existence, and yet outside the narrow limits in which we now exist we and our entire world are holograms. We are ethereal beings who live and work and learn in an insubstantial world. Pretty hard to picture, but the more you try to understand the new physics, the more it seems to make possible sense. This physical world was created as a schoolhouse for the purpose of draining the last ounce of knowledge and experience from every conceivable situation. Eventually we will all matriculate into our next adventure. And what will that one be? One can only wonder. Once I asked Romulus about quantum science and its concept that we and all our surroundings are holograms. This is what I was told.

> *As your science progresses you become more aware of a reality beyond your own reality. Energy can be formed into any shape and any meaning. Do you believe that you and your universe are the only forms energy takes? You are not. The God energy is total vastness waiting to be formed. Your world is contained between the vibrational limits that make up this perfection in which you exist. Other formed energy*

exists between different vibrational limits. Your physical world can use the same energy as other worlds but at a different vibrational level, and you are not aware of each other. The vibrational differences effectively make each of you invisible to the other. You and your world and everything else existing in and of the God energy are, as your science terms them holograms. The real part of your God existence is your unique spirit, the, "you", that is God created and can never be anything except perfect.

Chapter 10

Creating Your Own Reality

Most of us have heard or read that it's possible to create your own reality. But just how do we do that? Well, some people have the idea that others can do it for them. Some look for help and incentive from the other side, and so their whole life is spent waiting for a miracle. They never realize it's up to them to act, and the tools that will make their life better are already inside them, waiting to be used.

Many people expect the living to create the reality they want, perhaps a spouse, or parents or children. The only time that this seems true is in the first new flush of love, whether it's from a lover or at the birth of a baby.

Some expect that their work, their career, a beautiful home, and a fat bank account will provide the reality they crave. These, "Things", merely create your surroundings, your place in society, and you accept the half-full glass, always sensing that there is more but not understanding how to finish filling the glass to the top. Once you have achieved these things, they soon lose their luster and leave you thinking, "I have all that I dreamed of and it's not enough." So you look around and begin creating more of the same, thinking that this will bring the peace and fulfillment for which you have been searching, only to find that these new things are merely more Band-Aids that hide the truth. After awhile you realize that the longing for "Something More" is still there, as strong and demanding as ever.

So then, what is this satisfaction we crave, and how do we create it?

Somewhere deep inside your mind the answer is clear and waiting. Everything we do, think, feel, or react to is always recorded in a giant mass computer called the collective unconscious. This means that any experience of which we are a part not only records our handling of the situation, but that of everyone else who is involved.

We create who we are by the power we have to program our minds. If we allow our minds to dwell on such states as fear, hopelessness, anger, or any negative emotion, then that is what we become in life. We create our reality by the thoughts we believe about ourselves. The thoughts that we allow to grow create a cage that makes up our whole world. However, we possess the power to change these thoughts into their direct opposites: hope, love, trust, and faith. This power creates the day-to-day lives we live, and so thoughts wind up as our reality.

Keep in mind that we draw to ourselves from this collective unconscious these same thoughts that are forming our reality. The more of one emotion we put in, the stronger it reflects that emotion back to us, and that forms our reactions to life. This immense storage area holds the sum of all the knowledge and experience indelibly imprinted there from the self-imposed situations we create and react to. If you are living your life tied to the wheel of negativity, fear, anger, and hatred, and you are playing the victim, then this is what will be reflected back to you. However, if you react with thoughts and feelings of love, satisfaction, courage, and altruism, then these are what you will draw to yourself. The computer will always reinforce your life, not necessarily with what you need, but with what you request. Remember, though, this will lead to a limited experience of who you could be.

We always have the choice of how we will react to things that happen to us. Negative and positive experiences are opposites that are both made up of nothing more than basic energy. Also, to identify completely with either one produces limits that you will need to get rid of. By this, I mean that you can change your perceptions and map out an entirely different world for yourself by changing your day-to-day thinking. Remember, you are the boss and you can change your reality at any time. One of the major changes that humanity is bringing about is the ability to consciously create reality rather than unconsciously creating. Learning to do this will also eventually result in your changing the physical world and even re-creating your body—meaning you will have conscious control over your health, your aging, and your needs.

To find gratification you must search inward where your reality begins, where all the positive words apply. If you feel at ease with meditation, set aside a time each day to explore that part of yourself that is hidden. Let your thoughts flow gently in and out. Don't make judgments, and do not identify with any one thought. To do so gives the emotion of that thought power over your mind and begins the thinking process. Even to identify with a thought of awe and wonder leads you down the road of more thoughts and more thoughts, and soon you are reliving a whole incident. Just claim it as part of you and then let it go without internal comment. Once you give it importance and a name (anger, love, excitement), it then takes over your thinking. If you had a fight with your spouse that morning that was not resolved, the anger you felt will, if you allow it, fill your thoughts, and your session to find peace will be useless. Werner Heisenberg's uncertainty principle says that reality is observer created. Thoughts are energy like everything else, and when you observe and name a negative or a positive thought you give it power.

This reinforces what quantum theory puts forward; that thoughts are real things.

After a while you will begin to receive information that you instinctively know is your own deepest truth, information that you can use to better understand yourself and how you can bring changes to the areas of your life that you wish to change. This may seem uncomfortable at first and you may have doubts. Many times you will want to quit, but continue, and you will find that it is very much worth the effort when you begin to mine the gold that lies at your inner core. It is difficult to give a true picture of how to do it and what to expect because I believe that each personal truth is unique and each search for that truth is also unique. Your ultimate purpose is getting in touch with your Higher Self on a one-to-one basis, so if you hold that idea as your beacon, you can and will reach your goal.

If you are not comfortable with meditation, you need to keep track of your thoughts. Your inner self will send prompts known as intuition, and if you pay attention you can accomplish the same end as in meditation, that is getting in touch with your Higher Self. You must, however, learn to trust the intuitive thoughts and urges that arise in your mind. Trust is the element that will decide how soon and to what degree you will make a connection. Also, it matters how much of yourself you are willing to invest in this search. It must be, or become, very, very important to you.

You will, in time, come to the inner knowing that this is the way for you to connect. And connect you will. The intuitive urges will seem weak at first, but allow them credence and follow them. Let your trust build, let your faith in yourself strengthen, and as it does, you will begin to build a picture of who you really are. And that picture will be another step in reaching your Higher Self and becoming more than you were.

In this awakening to the new awareness that humanity is experiencing, we might wish for easy answers, and yet if we had our answers, there would be no purpose in searching for truth. Although we are all traveling toward the same enlightenment, we build unique paths as we go. If there were not an end toward which we are headed, both consciously and unconsciously, I can see no purpose to life other than putting ourselves in the same category as accidental bacteria.

My own mind was covered with many, many layers of prerecorded beliefs. As I stripped away these layers and smoothed the deep grooves that I had recorded throughout my life, I gradually succeeded in opening myself to my truth. Erasing these layers will pose a monumental task—believe me, I know—but it is a journey into uncertainty that, in time, will yield tremendous results.

As you journey further into your mind on the path to consciously meeting and communicating with your Higher Self, do not lose courage. At times the things you will discover hidden away in the closets of your mind will shame you, frighten you, perhaps even shock you, but continue, and I can promise that you will come to forgive and love who you are. Day by day you will be closer to discovering the self who lives quietly beneath the pain. The things that have shaped who you are rather than who you want to be will fade away. As they do, you will become aware of your Higher Self quietly waiting to take your hand, and your path will become easier.

Chapter 11

Free Will

To me, free will means that the future is never sure, because no matter what the situation, we always have choices. The basic choice of living or dying requires a definite decision. Should you decide not to make a choice at all, that also is a choice. The world we experience is created by our own consciousness. Nothing is done to us. Everything is done ultimately for our personal enlightenment. In blaming someone else for how you feel, you are saying that they control your source. By saying this, you are giving away your power.

Our destiny is in our own hands. We can recognize it and run to it with open arms and accepting minds, or choose not to. We can embrace it with expectancy and love, or we can choose to deny it, believing that we have no influence over the happenings in our lives. Either way our destiny is ahead of us; it is, in a way, already a part of us. Our progress can be speeded up by entertaining open-minded belief, or we can choose the longer route of emerging petal by petal into the light. Some crawl slowly and painfully because living in the shadows seems safer. But whichever path we choose, we will all finally emerge. Be assured that we are all destined to reach the light. This Earth life is a created shadow that we are painstakingly exploring, gaining every bit of experience that can possibly exist for our soul's becoming and for All That Is. Romulus spoke about this.

"You are beginning to come out of your shadow world
with the realization that spiritual growth begins as a stte of

mind. When you agree to entertain the truth that you are created from the energy of God then you will know that you are all one. The problems arise when you begin to think that you are better, worse, different or other and so are separated by religion, color, or place in societyRemember that the ones who live on the edges of the accepted rules society. You may hate the things that they do, but created from the energy that is God, then you will know that you are all one. The problem ari when you begin to to think that you are better worse, different, other, and so are separated by religion, color, or place in society. Remember that the ones who live on the edges of the accepted rules of society, the ones who kill and abuse are also as much created from the perfect God energy as you. You may hate the things that they do but you must love them as brothers and sisters created by the same God energy as yourself. They are involved in a self-chosen life that you either have already lived or will live in some other incarnation in order to offer your own unique version of it. Each spirit reacts to, and gains experience from, all conceivable situations. A new humanity will spring from the old as a plant springs from a seed bringing with it an, as yet, unperceived awareness. The past was the forerunner, the incubator of the marvelous future that lies ahead for humanity. Many are gathering here in awe to witness this new development. What you are doing has never been done. When humanity takes the reins of conscious creating, it will be a leap in its evolution that will lead to things that have never happened in the universe, You and those like you are opening the way, building the bridges, creating the path for all humanity to follow.

Chapter 12

The Magic of Love and Understanding

Forgiving does not mean forgetting. Each event in our lives, every situation to which we are called upon to react, is a chance to gain new experience, new knowledge, and above all, new understanding. Many of these happenings are painful, some are positively heartrending, and yet each was preplanned by all the spirits involved.

Most of the time we stick to the script we agreed upon before birth, but it is not written in stone that we do this. Each of us always has complete freedom to deviate from the plot at any time. If we stick to the script, we end life with the sure knowledge that we have gained what we needed and absorbed the joy and heartbreak and love we experienced. However, if we deviate from the preplanned actions, it creates no problems because there is no wrong way, and whatever direction we choose to take. we can do nothing but gain knowledge and experience. Sooner or later we will, again, plan a life to address the issue we tabled temporarily.

Many times we reincarnate among the same spirits with whom we have shared other incarnations. It can be as a family unit, friendship, business, or even as enemies. Before incarnation we all get together to plan life, this time in a situation that will allow everyone to gain the maximum of experience. How amazing it seems that before we come here, we love one another totally, and yet we set up situations where we can experience hatred, cruelty, murder, and victimization.

The most important thing we take away from every life is experience and understanding. We build on these themes life after life, and we grow, and as we continue our constant state of becoming so does ALL THAT IS, or GOD.

Chapter 13

Predicting the Future

In my mind, predicting the future is chancy at best. This is not to say that you cannot predict the future, only that you must choose which future looks to be the most likely based on what and where you are now. Every moment, you are presented with many choices as to which road to take. For example, if you visit a psychic for a reading, although she/he may have some ability and really try to help you. When the future is scanned a choice must be made from the many different possibilities based on your life as it is now.

Your choice at any given moment predicts the direction that your life will go, and if it matches what the psychic saw, fine, then it's "Wow, how did she/he do that?" If, however, the reading turns out to be wrong, you then doubt the psychic's words, not realizing that your future is a result of your own free will and that even you cannot predict your future with certainty. The psychic predicts what seems apparent at that time based on his or her reading of your possibilities.

As my contact with Romulus progressed, I had to say goodbye to many beliefs that I had held all my life. It was sometimes frightening, especially when it came to the beliefs that had seemed sacred to me. What I had believed about religion and God was frightening. How I pictured the world was even more frightening, but how I pictured my body and mind was the most difficult part to get around. We all grow up believing what we are taught, what we read, what we observe, and when we begin to discover that reality is not what we thought it is, to say the least, unnerving.

Romulus was very kind and gentle though. If I got upset over something

I was being shown, he would table it and wait to continue until I had gotten used to the idea.

The future is what we make it. We come into life with plans already laid out for that life, but we are free to change anything we wish at any time we wish. This is the major reason why a fortune teller cannot predict your future with certainty. The fortune teller is not in command. You are.

Chapter 14

I Learn to Cope with Reincarnation

As I became more and more familiar with the method of teaching that Romulus was using, I discovered that when the time came for me to begin a new area of learning, I would be given prompts. They came from here and there and everywhere. For example, I suddenly began to see references to reincarnation everywhere I looked. When it finally dawned on me that there was a purpose to these prompts I asked Romulus about it. He told me that it was time for me to get familiar with reincarnation and what it could do to help me in my present life. I was told to sit quietly and concentrate on wanting to remember a past life. Well, after umpteen tries, one day it came loud and clear. Not just one life, but several.

It wasn't like a movie. Each life was represented by one single scene. And as I saw these scenes in my mind each was accompanied by an emotion. I asked the purpose of what I was seeing and was told that each emotion was one that I needed to address in my present life. Some scenes showed me where I had helped people, while others brought home the knowledge that I have lived lives and done things that were hard for me to accept. But in all of them I felt again the pain or contentment, rage or joy, just as I had while living the life that they represented. I still carried the feelings from these lives somewhere inside myself and it was time to drain those emotions. I was being tormented in this life by pain that stemmed from fear and hatred emotions that were still directing me, dictating my life and eliciting the same reactions as when they had occurred. I was helpless in many situations because the events had happened when I was powerless to combat them and my subconscious was still reacting to similar incidents with the same negatives from the past that I wasn't knowledgeable enough to understand. I needed to know what prompted the situations in this life that I was reacting to in a negative manner and to recognize the times when I had found contentment. It brought a sense, almost, of tying up loose ends. The lives that had a bearing on my present one are as follows.

A life as a woman in ancient China held an overpowering sense of physical pain because of my bound feet. This woman had lived a mind-destroying life as a nonentity with no worth, and finally gratefully died. The abuse I had suffered in my present life made it impossible to overcome the low self-esteem from which I suffered until I began exploring this life.

The scene from a life as a ten-year-old boy, a black slave on a plantation, held a sense of wanting, yearning, needing. I was hiding at the edge of some trees and watching the white ladies and gentlemen coming down the steps of a beautiful house, and as I watched my heart ached because I knew it was something I could never have. I died before I reached my fifteenth year. This addressed my constant wishing for things I had no way of getting.

I was a Roman soldier and my brother Jim was my closest friend. We have had more than a few lifetimes together, and in this one we were companions in battle. From that life I learned the value of opening yourself up to someone close to you, of finding that unquestioned caring that develops between two people when trust is nurtured and proven.

I was a woman headed west on a wagon train who was respected because of her knowledge of herbal medicines. This one helped me begin to realize a better sense of self-worth and also explained where my long interest in herbal remedies had come from.

I was the wife of a sea captain standing on a high cliff during a terrible storm watching desperately for my husband's ship that was never to return home. This helped me to understand the feelings of anxiety and abandonment that had ruled me most of my life and were always seething just beneath the surface of my mind.

I was a woman, a member of the Essenes in the time of Jesus, tending a garden and looking off into the distance with a feeling of quiet stillness and total peace. That feeling of peace came through as a needed blessing to this life.

I saw a scene from ancient Japan where my life as a woman had been one of servile submission. It carried a deep hatred of men with loud shouting voices. That explained why, as long as I can remember, loud arguments and men shouting have always brought me to fear and anger.

Then I saw a scene where I lived in a cave and my life was a continual struggle for food and safety. I gloried in being outdoors and the sunlight made me happy. I gained a sense of innocent joy from this life that made me value the beauty of nature today in a way I had never done before.

These pictures and the overriding emotions they each carried were as clear as if I had just lived them, and they have remained forever imprinted in my mind. I found that most of these remembered lives pertained to some problem that had always held me back from socially interacting with others and from recognizing and coming to terms with the feelings of inferiority, insecurity, and unworthiness that had always ruled this life.

It took a long time and many applications of understanding before I gained much insight from them, but Romulus helped me. I was never told what to do or even how to do what I was working on, but after I had worked through a problem, I was always told that I had done well. It seemed that Romulus could help me ease into understanding on an unconscious level, but the conscious knowledge had to be lived through, thought through, and applied through my own conscious efforts.

I did prove that we have the ability to change our inborn conditioning. I was made to realize that due to the fact that everything is happening in total no-time, we can change our lives in the now by tuning into what we consider our past and future through meditation. In this way we become familiar with and experience every facet of this existence we call human. We are set up to react to every possible, every conceivable situation in order to absorb all of existence in the physical in our own unique way. This allows our soul to become more with every life and continues our becoming, which in turn enriches the becoming of ALL THAT IS, or GOD.

I was told that each bad experience that stays with you and affects your life is referred to as a burden. Now these burdens, if they are not resolved, are carried over from one lifetime to the next. In order to resolve a burden I was told you need to sit, comfortably relaxed, and bring up an event in your life that holds negative emotions. If you react very strongly, you can be pretty certain you are dealing with an emotion that is negatively affecting your life now. You must remember it as if it were happening right now.

Remember everything that occurred: the event itself, the smells, the sounds, the people involved. Allow yourself to totally feel the emotion. Let the hurt, the fear, the anger, the tears come. Just as these emotions affected you then, allow yourself to relive them now. It is very hard to do this, but you must review it over and over and over again, and after a while the negativity and hurt begin to ease until finally it seems as if you're watching a movie that happened to someone else. When you have done this, the negative emotions will be gone and no longer controlling your life. You remember them, but you don't feel them anymore. I did this over and over again, situation after situation (I was pretty messed up), and it not only worked, but the freedom it brought has allowed me to live a life that is no longer commanded by unresolved negativity.

Chapter 15

We Are Finally Growing Up

As time went on I was helped to understand every phase of life, along with my deepest questions. One day I began with this question: "Romulus, why is it that some people seem to be trying to find a way to learn about this quest for spiritual evolvement and others seem not to be aware of any possible changes at all, while still others call it impossible, insanity, or the work of the devil?" This is the answer I received.

> *Some of you are in the process of building new bridges across the chasm of forgotten limitations. You are, indeed, building the new awareness that humanity is now ready to bring into being, yet gain. You have reached this point in your evolution before and each time you have allowed yourselves to degenerate backward into the densness, the unenlightened state of being. This time you are determined to regain the knowledge of what being physical actually means; who you really are, where you came from, what your purpose is. You are gradually finding your way back to the, "knowing", that is your birthright. A great mind change is occurring that you have given yourselves permission to recognize. You are negating the self-built barriers tht you no longer need, the barriers that you yourselves erected in order to experience physical life in all situations. You allowed yourselve to forget who you are in order to pursue thee experiences and fulfill the ultimate purpose of your existence in physical reality which*

has always been to become more, and to grow through your unique responses. The next stage of human evolution is at hand and bridges must be built to cross the chasm between worlds. Barriers must be removed to allow for the mind expansion that humanity needs to reach the next stage. The ones who teach and explore beyond the normal are sensitives, These forerunners tread the path and build the common highway for all humanity to follow. You can each consciously and deliberately accelerate the the process of enlightenment by fostering your belief that the earth is not an end in itself but merely one step in your growth. Each step you take each individual gain you make benefits the whole of humanity. There is no, "right", way or, "wrong", way in the earth school. Each soul lives every facet of every situation, thus assuring that all possible knowledge will be explored. We guides, in harmony with humanity, are trying to bring world consciousness into a shift toward a more enlightened existence. Each person contributes to the mass awareness as they first make the conscious decision to seek truth and then strive to find the knowledge and understanding that their own special view of enlightenment brings. With each creation you bring about you must trust yourselves, trust your intuition, because those intuitive feelings are messages from your as yet, unrealized wholeness. To put your stamp on a truth is to face and solve a problem that exists in your life, problems you deal with in your own unique fashion. You have all lived many lifetimes in physical reality. That seems like a very long time to you, but it is such a small part of your ultimate destiny, Right now you are so much more than you believe and so much less than you will be.

As I absorbed this explanation, I began to value more the life I have lived this time around and the inner changes that I was living in the present. I realized that if my early life had been better (it was pretty bad), I might never have been brought to the point where I was contacted by Romulus. The very fact that he saved me from suicide by involving me in a new part of existence was, and still is, one of the most awesome and nearly unbelievable things to have occurred in this life.

I once asked him, "If I had not lived through the things that I have in this life, would I still have been contacted?" He replied:

> *"What we are doing is a part of what some others are doing to bring the new raised consciousness to the earth. As to whether we would have made this contact at some time is not known. You came into this life as part of a plan, but because others changed their part of of the original life, you were unable to do what you needed to do, You were at a point where you were ready to leave your life altogether. You saw nothing ahead in this life and were ready to leave when I offered you a choice. If you had not lived through the life you have you would not have been open to me, and perhaps you would not have been aware of me if I had tried. However you had the courage to grasp at the straw I offered. Once we cleared your past you have done so much with this life, and what we have brought into being helps others along the same road to knowledge that you have traveled.*

Chapter 16

Can Our Spirit Heal Our Body?

*I*n finding a way to open any of your chakras you must come to terms with the false beliefs you hold that are keeping them closed. Doing this is the most difficult task you will ever have, and the most rewarding to your spiritual journey. Gaining mastery over your own conscious beliefs is always painful, and the beliefs will intensify before they are finally mastered. You can hasten the process by examining your beliefs as they come into your conscious mind. The gaining of mastery over your own conscious beliefs will intensify before they are finally understood and become new personal truths. Question each as it rises into thought and consider and try out new ways to believe. You can create what you wish by the strength of your beliefs and the changes you are willing to bring to them. The physical world is the classroom and each spirits unique journey is the lesson. Remember, you must learn in order to teach and you must teach in order to learn. In this present evolutionary step you are trying to merge inner and outer realitiesl, and all humanity benefits by the small steps made by each individual spirit. Every time you come to a personal revelation it joins the mass consciousness and all spirits then have access to the knowledge.*

Chapter 17

Vibrations

After I had more or less absorbed the information on reincarnation, a later communication really set me to thinking out of the box. I had read about vibrations in books on quantum theory, so I expected Romulus to address the subject sooner or later. Now I don't claim to understand quantum physics, but I can grasp the theory that what seems solid in our world can, beginning with atoms, be reduced down to a basic energy that is the essence of everything. The way I understand solid matter, a house, an animal, a tree, our own bodies, everything in existence, is directed energy, vibrating at different resonances and resulting in the world as we perceive it.

We are now in a period of our evolution that calls for a tremendous leap forward, and we are in the process of doing just that. Now is the time when all humanity, and the very earth itself, are engaged in raising the common and individual vibratory rate to a higher level. This is occurring everywhere, and at ever-increasing speed. The reason for this constitutes the next step in humanity's evolving. We are now meant to become consciously aware of the self-set limits between our reality and the one just beyond. Becoming more aware will allow us to discover our next great adventure on the path of forever. As we are in the process of our own ongoing, "Becoming," so also is the energy that we refer to as God. Each problem that we address and solve, each breakthrough we make in our journey through forever, brings us further along our path of enlightenment. Each mortal's reaction to the situations they experience determines the myriad worlds of knowledge that are absorbed by ALL THAT IS, or GOD, or

TOTALITY, whatever name you personally feel comfortable with when thinking of your CREATOR.

Each day as I become more and more aware of truth, I change my outlook, my worldview, my actions and reactions toward myself and others. We are all matriculating out of this limiting reality and into the next step in our forever education. Some are moving at a greater speed than others, but know this: I am assured by Romulus that sooner or later we will all move on to the next step, ensuring a continuous, "Becoming".

Chapter 18

Re-joining Our Scattered or Splintered Selves into One

My life entered a period where I began to crave new things, things I had never experienced. A day came when I wanted to paint. I had never had any particular interest in painting and had absolutely no training in drawing. I had no idea how to bring together the tools I would need to begin. I knew nothing, and like the old saying, I didn't even suspect nothing. However, I blindly began to amass oil paints, canvases, and an easel; brushes, thinners, palette knives. Using a foam plate for a palette, I began to paint. Now, at first it wasn't good, but I seemed to know what to do to bring the effect I wanted, and soon I was painting nearly passable pictures. I will never be a great artist, but beginning with no training and little interest, I now possess the rudiments of the art.

Another time I sat at the computer and began to write poetry. Now I had never expected to be a poet. I wanted to write novels, and yet I seemed to understand how to write in any poetic genre I wanted to explore. Perhaps my poetry is not on the level of great poetry, but it is passable, I think.

One day I decided I wanted to explore gourmet cooking. This surprised me, because I had never had experience in using any spices except salt, pepper, and cinnamon. I did seem to have a talent for making pleasing combinations of foods and spices. I grew up on a backwoods farm, and our food was plain and simple, but I found that experimenting with new dishes was fun.

I finally got around to asking Romulus if there was a reason why I seemed to have a interest in doing things that I had never wished to experience before. He then explained about splintered selves. It seems that each reincarnational self is a splinter off the whole entity. Each historical self is a splinter. Also, each time we find ourselves in a situation that calls for several different paths, we splinter and go in different directions experiencing each different life. He said that I was, at last, bringing together my splintered selves, and when it was over I would, again, be a whole, complete spirit. Each self brings with it an area of expertise, and that is what I have been experiencing. He wound up with this statement:

> *Belief is the bridge that allows you to go beyond, to pass through your self-set limits. With your belief you have created the bridges that allow you to walk into your breakthrough. You have brought me and in a way I, too, am a self You have been bringing your many selves together and that accounts for your interest in the things that you wonder about. Each time a self is added you become a little more than you were----a newer human so to speak. You are not alone in your quest, and in time all humanity will bring the awareness that the few of you are creating now. All humanity will, as they understand and befriend their many scattered selves, become new humans. This reality you are living is only one of many futures that humanity could have chosen. Your world has chosen the path to awareness and enlightenment this time.*

In joining the splintered parts of ourselves again into one consciousness as we are meant to do, we are in the process of returning to the whole entities that we once were. The feeling of being more than I was is incredible. I have this part of me that is beautiful and powerful. I never realized that I was missing something until it was returned to me. What we are doing perhaps defies standing beliefs that have always been so dear to most religions. The belief that you are here and separate from your soul seems to be truth until you realize that you are never separate from your soul. Always we are connected, to each other, to our world, to our higher selves, to our souls, and thus to All That Is.

Humanity is now at the point in its evolution where this completion is our next step. As I have accepted my (more or less) lost selves, I am discovering many talents and interests I can now pursue. I accept what is happening with gratitude for the magic that has brought us together again as one. It is not as if I am invaded by strangers. It feels as if I am more than I was, but I am still "me."

Chapter 19

DNA

Because DNA has become a distinct part of our growing knowledge about who we are, I asked Romulus for his explanation, and this is what I was told.

The discovery of DNA is one part of the physical world that poses more questions than your science has, so far, been able to find answers for. Actually, they have identified only a small portion of your DNA, and what remains is thought of as useless by many scientists. Now ask yourself, when have you ever been aware of any creation that did not have a use? There is a wonderful and definite reason for every part of your DNA, First, DNA is who you are, the essential self. The small part that your science understands is what makes you the totally unique individuals that you are in your mortal lives. The larger part that science does not yet understand makes up your connection with your multi-dimensional forever selves. The part of you that is always aware, always bonded with your soul and thus always connected to your Creator. As this jump in human evolution that is now taking place brings its tremendous changes, the knowledge within your DNA will gradually be discovered. As humanity increases its awareness beyond the narrow limits of physical reality, it will gradually read and understand the book of DNA.

Chapter 20

What Lies Ahead for Humanity

O ne day I asked Romulus if our continuing incarnations were ever going to stop, and if so, were we going on to something else in our forever lives? He gave me this explanation.

> *Normal physical seeing keeps you stabilized in your reality. Consciously changing the way your eyes see will allow you to be aware of more while still staying grounded in the physical. If you believe what you see is real, then it is because you believe your eyes tell you is there. Your acceptance hinges on your belief, so you must change your beliefs to change what you see. You have lived with the limitations that you have imposed upon yourseves but now the time has come in your spiritual evolution when changing your beliefs will allow you to go beyond your self-set limits and become aware of what reality actually is. As you graduate from childhood and learn to become aware of what has always been just outside your comprehension, you will transcend the earthly lives you have known and matriculate into your next spiritual adventure. You have become so accustomed to your present state that you do not, as yet, really understand that you are so much more than you seem to be and so much less than you will be. As part of God and thus Gods in your own right, you grow with the experiences you gain from each life you live. As the Creator is limitless, your growth is also limitless, and thus your lives*

and experiences have have no limits. There are other places and other ways besides the physical that you can explore. It is always your choice where and what you decide to explore at any time. This forever trip that you are on is just that; forever. You should never fear what you look to as the future. There is no past or future as you think of it. No matter what happens, it is always, "Now". You progress and understand at your own speed. No one can do it for you. You are totally unique and there are no printed instructions; do this, do that, expect this effect as a result of that action. Each of you, in time, comes to the discernment that every realization brings change and every change always leads to another realization which leads to another change. As humanity progresses it encounters major evolutionary leaps, and one such is in progress now. You are in the process of raising your vibrations, which wil allow you to become aware of much more of the reality that your self-set limits now bar to you. You and many others are forging ahead and exploring for the benefit of all mankind. The very earth itself is raising its vibrations to facilitate this step that will bring about the, "New Human".

Tacitus said: "*The unknown always passes for the marvelous.*" The unknown will always remain marvelous and magical until we awaken and open our awareness. To do this, we must raise our vibrations and begin to understand what lies ahead in the tremendous now.

When can everyone experience the journey into the as yet unknown marvels that lie in our future? The first step is always to open your mind to realities beyond what religion has always taught. I am not saying that religion is wrong. It has comforted humanity for thousands of years. What I am saying is that there comes a time when we must go beyond the simplicity of the basic religious security blanket and give ourselves the freedom to accept an awareness that is only earned through opening our minds to other levels of reality.

I wind up this chapter with two poems I have written that, to me, explain our journey into forever. The first explains reincarnation, and the second tells the story of the journey we are on.

Goodbye My Love . . . 'Til Then

You and I will meet again.
One day in some other time and place I will sense you near,
and turning I will search you out in an alien face.
I will know it's you,
no matter what facade you will have chosen for the next adventure.
Your spirit will shine from eyes that,
though shaped or colored differently, will still hold the glow that is you.
The nature that has joined mine in so many adventures
will be apparent in the moment we pass,
and I will turn and see you, beloved soul friend, peering through those
eyes.
Somehow I will sense the precious spirit
that I have come to know and love through the ages we have been together.
Oh, the many times we have faced whatever life offered, together, always
together.
In our many relationships we have shared so much
that I will know you passing on the street, or across a concert hall,
or perhaps in the picture of a far-off place I will see your face.
So many times we've said goodbye,
but this time, my friend, I will merely say, "Til then,"
and await our meeting in another time, another place.
One day I will turn and see you, beloved soul, peering through strange
eyes,
but again illuminating my world with the glowing spirit that is uniquely you.

Shadow Of A Thought

Spirit born to learn from lives that quickly pass.
Wonderful elusive shadow flitting across the dimensioned screen of
mortality
playing out its chosen roles in time's great dramas.
Born into this world but not *of* this world,
evolving level by level, drama by drama,
always progressing in the attempt to understand love.
And in the end to exchange the finite for the infinite
in a world created by the one master intelligence.
Each consciousness finds its seat in Earth's great classroom,
coming back life after life to different climes
with different tools and different areas of skill
to pursue that next basic intent.
We pride ourselves on the extent of our knowledge,
and yet, answer this: Why are we here? Where are we from?
Who and what are we? Where we will go when we have mastered this class?
How do we measure the levels we strive to reach?
Are there other places, other realities, other classrooms,
and other subjects to master?
Of course there are,
and to ask, to wonder, to strive, to learn and experience,
is the first step in a human's maturing.
And the degree to which we progress in our quest
is the sign of a spirit seeking that elusive "something else"
that always lies just beyond the next personal revelation.

Jans Afterward

So, Jim and I have finally come to the end of this book and already I am feeling some nostalgia for the process of researching the subjects, and for the hours spent trying to put together the meaning of the message we bring you. Most of all I will miss the journey into my inner mind and the understanding that journey has brought to me. Really seeing my life through the aware eyes of reincarnation, along with the writing of this book has brought much greater insight that has consolidated into meaning about this tremendous odyssey humanity is on. This book has been a vision quest that I needed to bring the final inner consent to a project on which I have been working for some time. At any rate, whether I have the courage and inner strength to succeed or not, this life has been an extraordinary experience in becoming.

Jim and I have written this book with the deep and sincere hope that our readers will perhaps find some insight that will cause them to want to begin their own vision quest. If you allow yourself the freedom of thought to begin the voyage you will have taken a decisive step toward the tremendous future that Romulus has said lies ahead of humanity.

"God speed" and "Bon Voyage" my brothers. "Til we meet again.

Jans Acknowledgments

Every person with whom I have shared this incarnation has helped me through situations that held knowledge and enlightenment as a prize and my thanks to you all.

Thanks to my wonderful children for helping me to gain the understanding that I hold today.

I thank my brother Jim who has been my leaning post on this journey. He has lifted me up when I fell and had the courage and good sense to yank me back down when I flew too high.

I thank my dear friend Crystal Cassidy for her caring help with the computer problems I have had to deal with.

I thank my beloved sister-cousin Irene Bailey for the loving guidance and always being there for me to lift my spirits when I needed it.

Finally I give my heartfelt thanks to the entity called Romulus. The being who cared enough to take my hand and save me from a step that would have made the life changes and the enlightenment I have since gained impossible.

Romulus has consented to give a channelling to bring this book to its conclusion.

> *I will speak.*
>
> *Humanity has now passed a critical point in its evolution. Your earth world is raising its vibrations. You observe and are living through the painful upheavals that must be to bring about the changes tht are needed to assure the new worlds creation. As the earth is in upheaval so humanity is going through its own birth pangs to create the, "New Human". Do you think that there is not a reason for the turbulence that marks both the earths*

growth and mankinds evolvement? The last leap in evolution that was presented to humanity was when the Jesus Spirit came with the message of love and forgiveness. Did not that mark the gradual raising of human vibration? The time has now arrived when humanity is, again, rising to a new becoming. Many are gathering here to watch this birth with awe and such love. Do you not feel our joy? Do you not sense our wonder in watching you create a thing that has never before been created? Can you not be aware of the interest and excitement here that enthralls all who have been drawn to the emergence of the, "New Human". I tell you now that such a becoming as you are creating is shining as a beacon drawing many, many to witness your evolution. Do you wonder how this will bring such a difference of which you will soon become aware.? I will tell you just what I am able. The thing you do is something that has never been done and we cannot know what is not yet created. But this I can see. You are opening the portal to something that has been a potential for humanity. You are at the beginning of an exploration that will bring unheard of knowledge, and powers that you cannot yet imagine. You beautiful spirits have worked long and hard to achieve this new potential of raised vibrations. Your journey into, as yet, unexplored regions of becoming is now beginning and we are here to assist when we can. Since the beginning of your experiment in this reality you have shown such courage such a thirst for knowledge and becoming that we stand in amazement. We have respect for your courage in returning over and over to explore all facets of earth life for the good of all. You who read this book know that the journey into becoming is always yours to make, as is when you incarnate, where, and the spirits with whom you will incarnate. The spirits who have written this book have tried to share personal knowledge with you in the hope that the knowledge they have gained from their living and learning will awaken others to the path that all must take. I leave you with the certain knowledge that what is happening now has never been done. It is calling to all on this side, and know that your victory means so much more than you can realize.

About The Authors

The authors are siblings who, although separated in childhood, get together again later in life. They find that although one has lived a favorable life, the other has created the opposite. However they find that their beliefs and spiritual understanding are exactly the same. Anna has published one other book.